EDUCATION
LEAD(HER)SHIP

EDUCATION LEAD(HER)SHIP

Advancing Women in K–12 Administration

JENNIE WEINER

MONICA C. HIGGINS

HARVARD EDUCATION PRESS
Cambridge, MA

Paperback ISBN 978-1-68253-831-9

Library of Congress Cataloging-in-Publication Data is on file.

Published by Harvard Education Press,
an imprint of the Harvard Education Publishing Group
Harvard Education Press
8 Story Street
Cambridge, MA 02138

Cover Design: Ciano Design
Cover Image: lushik/DigitalVision Vectors via Getty Images

The typefaces in this book are Candide and Neue Haas Unica.

Contents

Foreword

When I published my first journal article in 1976, I was in the first year of my PhD program, having left a teaching position at a K–12 independent school in New York City to pursue a doctorate. When I entered my PhD program and announced my intentions to become the head of a K–12 girls school, I was told that I didn't have a chance. No one would ever hire me. First, they said, I was an open, gasp, feminist. Moreover, I was a woman. I just wouldn't do. I was advised to think about preparing for a professorship, although I probably wouldn't get a job in a university either. So I became a professor. I didn't even try for an administrative position.

It wasn't as if I didn't have any idea of the barriers facing women in school administration. That first article, written with Pat Palmier, was entitled "Up the Front Staircase: A Proposal for Women to Achieve Parity with Men in the Field of Educational Administration."[1]

I continued to research women's leadership in the nearly five decades since. It's hard to write that sentence because fifty years seems like sufficient time to have solved the "problem" of women's underrepresentation in school leadership. But here we are. And that's why this book, written by two researchers with years of experience, is necessary.

There has been much excellent scholarship that defines, explains, and describes the barriers facing women. More has been written about White women, but a strong body of scholarship about the experiences of women of color in school administration is growing. But, still, here we are.

Jennie Weiner and Monica Higgins have produced a book that transcends what is available in the field and which has the potential to propel actual change. Both authors are deeply grounded in independent school and public school education, organizational theory, and intersectionality scholarship. They bring their expertise to the problem we thought we had solved—women's lack of proportional representation in school administration.

This intersectional analysis of women's leadership examines more closely the system and structures that shape "women's experience in K–12 education leadership and considers a better path forward." Through the voices of both aspiring and current leaders, Weiner and Higgins tell their stories, providing the reader with what Rudine Sims Bishop refers to as "windows, mirrors, and sliding doors" to allow "female education leaders to see themselves, their experiences, and their value in this space and give others, who do not have such identities, insights into these experiences."[2]

Weiner and Higgins map the ways that the teaching profession is treated as a semi-profession of tireless volunteer workers who are expected to go the extra mile or ten with little pay, support, or chance for advancement. Their discussion is framed within the context of women's paid work and women's work as family members and caretakers. They also provide insights into the racialized differences in these expectations and frameworks. The women leaders who speak in this book tell the tale of benevolent sexism within the expectations of women's emotional work, both at home and in the workplace. This emotional labor is not only invisible in formal systems, but it also forces women to show emotions that are "incompatible with their true feelings," leading to emotional exhaustion. And, if that isn't bad enough, such behavior, although expected, is not defined as leadership.

The case studies of the women leaders are wonderfully illustrative of the emotional work expected, even as they are depressingly repetitious of similar descriptions shared in my five decades in the field. This is a comment not on the authors of this book, but on the lack of progress made to support and nourish women's leadership.

We fail to count the cost and importance of emotional work as a leadership ability. We also unfairly burden women with the time, patience, and energy it takes to listen, support, and encourage. We know from research that when teachers and parents come to a male administrator, they apologize for taking his time and make sure they keep their remarks short. This is unlike the ways in which women administrators are approached and expected to sit, listen, respond, and be supportive. The issue isn't that emotional work is extraneous. It's that it isn't counted as leadership. And it's work that is expected of women but not of men.

The stories of women's lives in this book make it clear how hard they work and how well qualified they are. And yet they are sabotaged by actors within the system. Not only are they smart and hardworking, these women spent many more years as teachers, instructional coaches, and curriculum developers than their male counterparts who enter administration. They come more fully prepared to support instruction and growth. But this advantage is often used against them.

Principals who don't want to lose a reliable, successful teacher often provide mixed messages about a move into administration, partly for the self-interest of the principal. As one principal scolded when hearing that his prize teacher was hired to lead a new STEM school, "I can't believe that after all we've done for you, you are leaving us high and dry. We need you, the kids need you, and you're leaving." Women can't count on support as they move up and through administration. What they can count on is being made to feel guilty for leaving.

Throughout this book, for each of the cases presented, Weiner and Higgins move through and beyond telling the story. They provide a structure for thinking of alternatives, responses, and ways forward. The questions to consider for each case and the themes that emerge offer a pathway to think about systemic and personal change. A good example is their analysis of care work. Teachers and instructional coaches who do a lot of "care work," but without an additional title, often take longer to get a position in administration because they have "nothing" on their resumes that captures this leadership contribution. As the authors note, "none of the events in these cases [about care work] should have felt out of step with everyday work in schools and school systems. In the education field, overwork and care work are normalized." But care work can be valued and does represent leadership and skill. The authors provide ways to disrupt the normalization of women's care work, change the system to support care work, and put it on the leadership ladder.

The authors interestingly examine what counts as leadership, pointing out that leadership is socially constructed, particularly around gendered roles. More collaborative approaches are often seen as weak. Men's missteps are more likely than women's to be chalked up to gaining experience than to lacking leadership ability. The intersection of race and gender continues to disperse and complicate understanding of leadership behaviors.

Within the cases, the reader will notice that many of the women are divorced and/or single parents. This is not unusual. Male administrators are much more likely than female administrators—at all levels—to be married. Unlike women who are more likely to be handling all home and work tasks without the help of a partner, male administrators have partners who do the care work, leaving them free for work and leisure.

The stories ring true because they are true. There are few women administrators who won't nod a head in recognition. What is different about this book are the questions for discussion and thought, the exploration of themes across cases, and the ways to think about changing the organizational patterns.

For example, women's varied experiences of role incongruity across the stories illustrate how clashing expectations work against women. To confront and disable these expectations, Weiner and Higgins offer approaches such as anchoring that address incongruous expectations, such as the tug and pull of being liked or being competent.

The strategies provided aren't only for the woman leader. They are also for the supervisor, suggesting ways to restructure, rethink, and supervise more effectively. These cases and the examination of alternative behaviors and thought processes are exactly what administrative preparation programs should be teaching those preparing to be school administrators—whether male or female.

"They only call on us when nobody else will say yes." This woman's story is an apt description of the schools and jobs women are often "offered." This is particularly true for women of color. In other words, gatekeepers turn to women of color as well as White women when the organization is falling apart. The exploration of breaking the glass ceiling only to discover a glass cliff is explored through the experiences of three women of color. All three were brought into troubled, dysfunctional systems without support. All three had strong commitments to the populations which these schools served, and all three increased student success along with other positive reforms. And yet all three were undermined, blocked, and betrayed by those who hired them. They were committed, savvy, and effective leaders. They also experienced the glass cliff. Using their experiences, Weiner and Higgins provide strategies to disrupt the glass cliff and reimagine the organization.

Racial and gender microaggressions are aimed at nearly all women who step out of their lane. School administrators are no exception. The experience of microaggressions and the effect on women school administrators is examined in three case studies. The structures and practices of organizations that permit and even encourage microaggression are dissected. These daily mini-traumas are both gendered and racialized, and women are expected to ignore them and move on.

The role of anger is examined as a strength, rather than a shortcoming, when facing the realities of a less than supportive environment. Instead of urging women to suppress or ignore their anger, Weiner and Higgins suggest how to use anger to build and change.

This book is the most useful and focused treatment of women's experiences in school leadership and administration that I have come across. Framed within an empirical and theoretical structure, women's stories illustrate and illuminate the gendered and racialized expectations of emotional labor, role congruity theory, the glass cliff, and the many ways that women are sacrificed to the organization.

The questions and discussion encouraged by the authors are not just for women aspiring to or enacting leadership roles. They are for the organization. What should the organization be doing to create an environment that corrects for the gendered and racialized barriers that go unchallenged and unstopped? Weiner and Higgins speak to supervisors and urge them to examine themselves and then to intervene to change the culture. Useful and doable strategies are proposed both for women moving into leadership and for others in the organization whose job it is to ensure a fair and just environment.

I can easily imagine using this book in the classroom as well as in professional development workshops. Grounded in theory but presented through compelling and real stories of what women in the first part of the twenty-first century are experiencing will energize and teach.

The disappointing and sad fact is that the experiences of women school administrators and leaders, although better in some ways, aren't that much different than what I wrote about nearly fifty years ago. The gift of this book is that the authors don't just chronicle women's experiences, they provide a pathway for readers, working together, to resist and thrive. Weiner and Higgins understand that each woman's experience might be an individual story, but together they are a history of lost contributions. These stories indict school organization leaders for failing to justly manage and profit from the leadership, caring, and excellence that women represent.

Charol Shakeshaft, PhD
Professor, Educational Leadership
Virginia Commonwealth University
School of Education

CHAPTER ONE

A Focus on Women in K–12 Education Leadership: Why This Book?

Despite women being overrepresented as public school teachers, they are underrepresented in leadership positions. In 2018, women held more than 75 percent of all teaching positions, but only 54 percent of principal positions.[1] Moving up the ladder of education leadership, women's representation becomes ever more meager: in 2018, only 27 percent of superintendents were women. These numbers are even starker when we consider the experiences of women of color. For example, in that same year, only 6 percent of principals in US public schools were Black women, and only 2 percent of superintendents identified as African American. The number of women within that group was difficult to ascertain as the same national education database had failed to disaggregate this information for public use—a signal, perhaps, of the lack of interest in addressing these inequities.[2]

Consistent with women's experiences in the workforce more broadly, the reasons for this underrepresentation are complex and multifaceted, stemming from issues as diverse as women's willingness or ability to merge their work and family responsibilities, to inequitable hiring practices that reward men's potential over women's competency, to how we conceptualize leadership itself.[3] A lack of female mentorship and, as seen in a harsh light during the COVID-19 pandemic, policies that often fail to support working women and their care duties can also serve as powerful barriers to women's leadership opportunity. Together, these elements can create what Herminia Ibarra, Robin Ely, and Deborah Kolb call "second generation gender bias" in which discrimination becomes more invisible or hidden in the organizational structures, norms, and systems, normalizing the absence of women in leadership roles, while simultaneously promoting problematic and inaccurate discourses that women lack the desire, capability, or confidence to engage in such roles.[4]

Work highlighting such discrimination and the gendered (and racialized) nature of K–12 school leadership continues to be treated as peripheral and has yet to be taken up at scale by schools, school systems, or education leadership programs.[5] Moreover, when, in the rare times that the research does address these issues, it often presents them as atheoretical or framed with theories that lack criticality regarding gender discrimination. Alternatively, work has focused on gender differences in whether and how female leaders' approach to leadership (shared leadership, social justice leadership, instructional leadership) aligns with that of male colleagues.[6] Finally, a small but growing body of work has focused on how education leaders' identity (most often their racial identity) relates to their interactions with students and families.[7] In our reviews of the literature, however, we have not yet seen much on what it means to be a woman leading in the space or how educators, parents, and students might treat these women in their roles.

This same oversight persists in education leadership programs. Indeed, when Jennie taught a course on women and education leadership at Harvard's Graduate School of Education in the fall of 2020 (the inspiration and testing ground for the ideas in this book), it was the first and only course at the school centering gender in leadership and introducing theories of how gender discrimination plays out in leadership more broadly. It was also overenrolled, suggesting pent-up demand for such topics. Moreover, this gap regarding opportunities to build understanding in how gender discrimination affects women's experiences in education leadership is pervasive across the field. We have talked with and studied hundreds of female education leaders over the years, and few could recall any professional development opportunities or books that expressly discussed what it meant to be a woman leader in education, spoke explicitly about or provided theories to frame gender discrimination in the space, or addressed ways to cope with or disrupt it when it happened.

When resources that focus on women and leadership are available, they tend to exist outside the field of education and advance one of two messages:

- To be successful, female leaders need to take on the attributes of male leaders (bold, strong, aggressive) and "lean in."
- Female leaders are more effective because of their ability to embrace and use their "female" characteristics (care, collaboration, shared governance) to support organizational learning and performance.

Unfortunately, both orientations, although perhaps well-intentioned, are grounded in stereotypes about who women are and should be. Moreover, instead of providing theories that would help women see patterns of discrimination and give language to experienced phenomena, these "solutions" place the problem of gender discrimination at the feet of women and ask them to outperform bias (an impossible feat).

These resources are also often mute on the topic of race and how gender intersects with other forms of identity to affect how women of different racialized and other identity features (e.g., sexuality, disability status, class) experience the world. Instead, we need work that operates from an intersectional perspective, uplifting the fact that race, gender, ethnicity, and other identities "operate not as unitary, mutually exclusive entities, but as reciprocally constructing phenomena that in turn shape complex social inequalities."[8] Indeed, intersectionality calls attention to social identities that often are treated as marginal, while simultaneously highlighting the "complex nature of power" and its manifestations in everyday life.[9] In so doing, intersectionality pushes us to move away from centering Whiteness and maleness (among other dominant identities) and instead to consider the unique and complex nature of an individual's lived experience.[10]

As Ella Bell Smith and Stella M. Nkomo highlight in their book *Our Separate Ways*, such an orientation serves not to "suggest that one group of women experienced greater or less challenges in the workplace, but rather to illuminate the specific nature of the barriers as perceived by the women themselves."[11] Women leaders of different backgrounds need resources that uniquely speak to their lived experiences and that give them greater insight into those of their sisters in new ways. We hope this book will serve as one of those resources.

On this note, it is important to name our positionality as two White women, and how Whiteness has shaped our perspectives and orientations to this work—an essential element of engaging an intersectional framing as White scholars. We have our own set of blind spots and misconceptions that we have worked to continually and proactively interrogate and attend to.[12] In so doing, we hope to reclaim a true feminist framework in which we uplift and celebrate both the differences and similarities of those who identify as women. As Gloria Steinem said in a recent talk we attended, "If it's not intersectional, it's not feminism"—an adage we hope to live up to.[13]

THE STRUCTURE OF THE BOOK

This book seeks to challenge traditional discourses about who female education leaders are and what they should be and to provide readers with an opportunity to learn about and analyze the systems and structures shaping women's experiences in K–12 education leadership and consider a better path forward. Such work is needed to blend theory and practice and help create what Rudine Sims Bishop, in her research on representing diverse stories in children's books, refers to as windows, mirrors, and sliding doors—that is, opportunities for current and aspiring K–12 female education leaders to see themselves, their experiences, and their value in this space and give others, who do not have such identities, insight into these experiences.[14]

As we have highlighted, this book is meant to be a practical resource that names how gender discrimination and gendered racism exist and operate within the education leadership pipeline, how they affect women's leadership trajectories and experiences, and how to disrupt these forms of discrimination.[15] To do so, each chapter is designed to, first, share information about theories of gender discrimination and their applicability to education leadership (i.e., the window). Next, we invite readers to see and reflect on, through cases based on female K–12 education leaders' experiences in the field, how such discrimination is operationalized in their everyday lives. We include discussion questions for each case as an opportunity for community and self-reflection about these topics and their applicability within your own context (i.e., the mirror).

Indeed, one of the drivers for this book has been our commitment to provide an opportunity for women in education leadership and those interested in supporting them to see their or others' experiences as part of a larger pattern or phenomenon. We came to this conclusion after years of facilitating women's leadership sessions in which, after explaining these theories and giving some examples, participant after participant would share similar stories from their own lives, opening with something like, "I thought it was only me" or "The same thing happened to me!" Such experiences illustrated not only the lack of opportunities K–12 female education leaders had to come together and openly share their experiences but also the gaps in their knowledge about gender discrimination more broadly and its impact on their ability to see the forest for the trees (or in this case, the institutional nature of the everyday, commonplace discrimination they faced).

Finally, at the end of each chapter, we consider possible paths forward as well as ways to challenge and disrupt this discrimination in situ (i.e., the sliding doors). It is important to differentiate between providing opportunities to engage in learning and change and giving prescriptive how-to's on addressing institutional bias. We believe we can offer tools for those on the ground to engage in the hard work of reflection, capacity building, and action; however, we do not suggest that we can solve gender discrimination in education leadership with any one resource or any one approach. We need everyone for this job; this book is merely a beginning step to bring us together.

CONTENTS

We begin this journey in chapter 2, "The Undervaluation and Overreliance on 'Women's Work,'" by giving an overview of the historically gendered nature of the teaching profession and its relationship to the type of care work and emotional labor female teachers and then leaders are expected to do. Specifically, we narrow in on the phenomenon of emotional labor and highlight the ways women must often display care, calmness, and agreeableness and complete additional tasks to keep their workplaces running smoothly, regardless of their true feelings or aspirations to do so.[16] A key element of emotional labor is the burden it places on women to ignore or sublimate their emotional needs.

In the context of schools, educators often are asked to provide emotional labor in the service of caring for their students and families.[17] Such realities are salient across the education continuum, with women and women of color, specifically, holding most of the care or "service" work in academic settings while simultaneously experiencing negative consequences, whether informal (disrespect, devaluing) or formal (poor performance ratings, being passed over for promotion), as a result.[18] With that said, and despite its ubiquity, emotional labor is often invisible (absent from roles and responsibilities, hiring criteria, and merit structures); instead, it is assumed as "natural" for women, oftentimes with negative impacts on women's financial well-being and organizational status.[19]

Finally, we would be remiss not to mention the ways these concepts of emotional labor bleed over from women's work to their home lives and how the latter affects the former. For example, Ellen W. Eckman found that male principals felt their ability to function effectively was largely due to their wives' role as primary caretaker of their children.[20] In contrast, women often highlighted the professional sacrifices they made for their families as they moved into education leadership roles.

In chapter 3, "The Double Bind for Women Leaders," we introduce the framework of social role theory. This framework highlights the double bind that many women in K–12 education leadership experience as they attempt to negotiate being either "too soft" or "too hard" in order to succeed in these roles.[21] Specifically, social role theory proposes that expectations exist regarding the roles men and women fill in society. These expectations focus on the roles men and women should occupy (prescriptive roles) as well as the qualities and behavioral tendencies stereotypically demonstrated by each gender (descriptive roles). Within these constructed expectations, women are often described as holding communal attributes, such as being affectionate (emotive), helpful, and nurturing, and these communal attributes are perceived as most appropriate for women to demonstrate.[22] Conversely, men are often described as holding agentic attributes, such as being aggressive, dominant, and self-confident, and these attributes are perceived as most appropriate for men to demonstrate.[23]

At the same time gender is constructed, so too are professional norms and ways of understanding a job or occupation. This includes leadership, which has long elevated, in education and elsewhere, the concept of a "lone hero"—that is, a strong, charismatic, innovative, and ambitious individual. The description of leadership tends to favor traditionally stereotyped agentic qualities (male characteristics) and disfavor those seen as stereotypically female.[24] This alignment of stereotypes helps to explain why men are often cultivated to take on leadership roles and women are seen as not possessing "leadership material."[25]

When women are granted access to leadership, they often face a dilemma: they can act in ways that are associated with leadership (agentic) and conflict with stereotypes of female behavior, or they can act in accordance with female stereotypes (communal) and conflict with leadership expectations. Such conflicts then evoke backlashes as women face criticisms for being either too aggressive when agentic or too emotional when communal—criticisms that manifest in everything from performance evaluations to compensation to a general sense that women are held in poor regard as leaders.[26]

In chapter 4, "Shattering the Glass Ceiling and Landing on a Glass Cliff," we shift to the phenomenon associated with gender discrimination in which, women, when finally granted access to leadership, are disproportionately charged with orchestrating dramatic turnarounds, often without adequate resources to succeed.[27] Moreover, when women are not successful in such conditions, it is more likely to be attributed to their gender; in contrast, when a man is successful in such a role, he is more likely to be given outsized credit.[28]

Although most of the research regarding the applicability of the glass cliff in education has been conducted in higher education, there is suggestive evidence that it fits with the experience of women in the K–12 space as well.[29] For example, we already know that women, and women of color in particular, are more likely to be placed in the neediest schools with the poorest performance relative to their male colleagues.[30] Beyond placing them in these more difficult conditions, they are also positioned in such spaces as "cleanup" women,[31] meant to act as change makers under tremendously difficult and often undersupported conditions. Moreover, and even despite the lack of success others may have in turning situations around, female leaders in such settings often face high levels of scrutiny, criticism, and blame, putting them at greater risk of "failure" and facing greater consequences.[32] And yet, as the only chances for leadership often come in schools and districts that are or are perceived to be teetering on a cliff, aspiring female leaders may feel compelled to take on such positions to have a chance to lead, no matter the potential costs to their careers.

In chapter 5, "Gendered (Racial) Microaggressions and Death by a Thousand Cuts," we discuss gendered and gendered racial microaggressions and their impact on female education leaders. Microaggressions are the "brief and commonplace daily verbal, behavioral, or environmental indignities, whether intentional or unintentional, which lie beneath visibility or consciousness and which communicate hostile, derogatory, or negative slights and insults."[33] Although much of the literature on microaggressions has focused on race specifically, there is growing consensus and research that they are also perpetrated on women, members of the LGBTQI+ community, and others of minoritized identities, occurring in distinct and intersecting ways and in schooling environments. Work examining microaggressions specifically in the context of education leadership is somewhat sparse (with few exceptions),[34] but they regularly do occur and need to be understood as symptoms of institutional bias and not simply as rudeness or incivility.

Additionally, failure to consider intersectional frameworks when trying to understand women's experiences in education leadership can lead to blind spots in addressing discriminatory systems and structures. For example, the dearth of Asian American and Pacific Islander (AAPI) female superintendents may not only be an issue of gender but also of race. The microaggression AAPI individuals experience of being treated as the other or as "strangers in their own land" contributes to a sense of dehumanization and discourages full participation in educational structures.[35] Policies that solely work to diminish gender bias (e.g., quotas or mentoring programs) may continue to create predominately White spaces and thus fail to address structures and beliefs that would help AAPI or other female leaders of color to fully thrive.

In our conclusion, chapter 6, "What Now?," we speak to how readers might use this book to incite action at different levels of their organizations. This includes thinking about how we might exert agency in discriminatory systems as well as the role men can play as allies in the fight for gender equality and the role White women can play for racial equity and intersectional feminism. We end with calls for increasingly expansive conversations about gender discrimination to encompass all the varied identities women hold and the relationship of these identities to leadership.

CONCLUSION

Systems and structures have existed for years that create tremendous barriers to success for women in leadership, but we do not believe this is a fait accompli. Women are keen on understanding these systems and structures; this book can help them do that. We also hope this book provides a resource for more than just those women who have experienced these barriers and are looking for solutions. Beyond our "target audience" of aspiring women in K–12 education leadership, we hope to reach those who work with women, who work for women, and who women work for. Change is abetted by connection and community; by providing opportunities for collective understanding across racial, ethnic, and other identity markers, we hope to connect women through a sense of sisterhood. Finally, we want this book to offer insight to people who face barriers that do not stem from gender-based differences. As the research shows, issues associated with microaggressions, to name just one issue we explore, are not limited to women. By sharing insight from a multiplicity of fields, we hope to give some language, concepts, and frameworks to help a wide range of people better understand their true felt experiences in this space we call education leadership.

Of course, concepts and frameworks are only as good as they are useful. For this reason, we offer stories from the field so you can see these ideas in practice. Then, using the provided questions for reflection, you can decide what is or is not meaningful to you. We did not write this book to sell any particular concept or framework, but rather to improve understanding, which is the prerequisite to action. What rings true for you is personal; how you act and bring about change, however, will affect the course of careers beyond your own. Despite our human bias toward action—and even though leadership is indeed all about action and change—it is still crucial to know what the problem is that you are trying to solve and, further, to thoughtfully diagnose its root causes. The concepts and stories in this book can provide the pillars for your own thoughtful diagnoses, along with shared felt experiences that, we hope, will undergird your rationale for action, whether that be collective or individual. We aim to help aspiring female leaders to be even more intentional in their actions, to recognize they are not alone, and to inform and, yes, persuade others to take action to unravel the inequities that continue to block rightful leadership for women in K–12 education.

CHAPTER TWO

The Undervaluation and Overreliance on "Women's Work"

I knew all the informal coaching I was doing was keeping me from doing my best with my students, but, honestly, I didn't feel like I could say no and still be considered a "team player."

—FRANCESCA (TEACHER LEADER)

I worked so hard to get us all, me, my husband, and the kids, to a place where I could step back a bit at home and get to lead. I can't believe I just had a position offered to me and taken away because I'm the mom of two teenage girls.

—JO (ASSISTANT SUPERINTENDENT)

When I finally told my principal I got a job as the leader at the other elementary school, he was super upset. He kept telling me what a great job I was doing with our "frequent fliers" and everyone would miss me so much. He was saying "please don't leave" until the last day.

—MARIA (PRINCIPAL)

INTRODUCTION

It is often the case that becoming knowledgeable about a contemporary issue (e.g., racial injustice, immigration policy, climate change) is
contingent on knowing the historical context of how that issue evolved.
Women's access and ability to thrive in education leadership is, in this
way, no different than any other pressing issue of our time. Indeed, the
status of women in the profession is a function of systems and structures
within and outside the field of education that continue to endure. To
understand some of the key reasons women today have difficulty accessing and thriving in education leadership, it is necessary to understand
two intertwined and longstanding issues: (1) women's overrepresenta-
tion in the teaching profession but underrepresentation in education
leadership roles (education being a feminized profession), and (2) the
continued undervaluation of care work in schools, school systems, and
our larger society.[1] These issues are the rotten fruit of the same poisonous
tree—patriarchy and the devaluation of work that is deemed feminized
in our society.[2]

As we will discuss in more detail, this framing helps explain why
teachers continue to be treated as part of a semiprofession. It's why
educators are consistently asked to do more and give more. They're
called heroes, but they are rarely paid in accordance with their effort
and skills or treated with the dignity and respect they deserve. It is also
why those who do the most for schools by giving their time and energy
to support others are often passed over for promotion or are seen as too
emotional or weak to lead. It's no coincidence that women and women
of color engage in more care work in their organizations than their male
colleagues and that their work is undervalued.[3] As a note, when we say
"care work," we mean everything from more explicit efforts taken to
create an organizational culture in which people feel connected and valued (e.g., mentoring, organizing celebrations, induction) to those more
informal "off-the-clock" efforts that make the organization run smoothly
(e.g., making sure there are snacks at meetings, helping families after

hours with immigration paperwork, or counseling a coworker going through a divorce).

To help explain why this is the case, how we got here, and the relationships among feminization, care, and education leadership, we begin with a general overview of many contemporary women's experiences in the workforce. We then shift to teaching as a feminized and White profession, and how this shapes the valuation and nature of educators' work and women's access and ability to thrive in education leadership specifically.

WOMEN IN TODAY'S WORKFORCE

Today's generation of women has the highest labor force participation in history.[4] At the same time, research shows that women today work more hours outside the home and in it than they did in 1965.[5] Indeed, despite their ever-expanding roles in the world of work, women continue to hold most of the home and family-based labor (housekeeping, childcare, schooling, elder care).[6] This phenomenon is often called the second shift—women clock out of a long day of work only to clock in at home.[7] "As masses of women have moved into the economy, families have been hit by a 'speed-up' in work and family life. There is no more time in the day than there was when wives stayed home, but there is twice as much to do. It's mainly women who absorb this 'speed up.'"[8]

The result of such distribution is that women generally have less leisure time than men and worry more about meeting the expectations of home and work.[9] In our experience, working women are barraged by questions about how they achieve work–life balance (spoiler: they don't, because it's impossible to manage giving 100 percent in both places), whereas men are rarely asked these questions. Analyzing the reasons for this difference a bit more critically, we argue that the failure to ask men how they can "have it all" is grounded in a belief that it's natural for men to focus on work more than home, as presumably someone else is attending to domestic issues. In contrast, it's a problem for women to make such a calculation because it is assumed that their household will fall apart in their absence. The fact that such questions and the associated gendered distribution of labor continues today suggests a need to radically reimagine work, the family unit, and the role of male partners in domestic life.

On this note, while this framing is heteronormative in terms of a family unit being composed of a man and woman, the undervaluation of home and family care is true even in same-gendered couples. Indeed, researchers find that one spouse frequently holds more of what might be deemed the more stereotyped feminized caregiving roles and these roles are subsequently devalued in the household because they are deemed to be more female.[10] Single mothers, too, a growing proportion of parents, fully take on this domestic work and face distinct and stacked challenges negotiating their work and home lives, frequently facing harsh and undue criticism when some part of this unmanageable role slips.[11] Single women without children also face expectations about their caregiving responsibilities, particularly when it comes to attending to aging parents or siblings with medical or other needs, or expectations from their employers that they can simply fill in the gaps that others with families are deemed too busy to engage in.[12] Whatever women's sexual identity or partnering situation might be, such work is exhausting, often depleting, and is simply not being taken up by men to the same extent and at scale.

This double standard was in stark relief during the COVID-19 pandemic. As schools shuttered, women, because of gendered and racialized work patterns, faced particularly difficult circumstances.[13] Part of this difficulty stems from the gender pay gap. According to the *2022 State of the Gender Pay Gap Report,* all women make, on average, $0.82 for every $1.00 White men make, while Black women make $0.79 and Hispanic women make $0.78 against the same $1.00.[14] As a result of these lower wages and women's central role in domestic work, large numbers of women felt forced to leave their positions to care for children at home and stepped out of promotion or leadership pathways.[15] Other women, because of their clustering in service professions (hospitality, cleaning, nursing, elder care), were either laid off or, when such positions were categorized as essential, they took on the burden of the work and faced the danger of the pandemic, while continuing to be the primary caregiver at home.[16]

Such hardship was true as well for educators, many of whom had young children of their own and were called to return to school.[17] And yet, while many parents voiced their desire to have teachers attend to their children, little attention was paid to teachers' inability to access affordable and high-quality childcare for their children or healthcare for other family members or loved ones who required support. Such responsibilities align with the long-held belief that teachers have special care responsibilities. As we discuss next, this belief is rooted in the feminization of the profession and barriers to women's access to leadership roles as a result.

FEMINIZATION OF THE TEACHING PROFESSION

As we talk a bit about the history of the teaching profession, it's important to name that this history is racialized. As schools proliferated and White women became the solution to the heightened demand for teachers during the common schools movement beginning in the 1830s and beyond, atrocities were perpetrated on people of color and their communities across the nation.[18] Slavery remained the norm in much of the United States, with threats of death for those enslaved even learning to read.[19] Indigenous children were taken from their families and forced to acculturate to White norms of behavior. Similar fates met Hispanic, Asian, and other racialized or ethnically minoritized children and their families as they entered schools built for White people that violently propagated White norms. There are many powerful stories of resistance during this time and beyond, resistance that was often led by women of color who created spaces and fought to elevate the genius of their children;[20] overall, however, the story of public education is steeped in Whiteness and White Supremacy as much as it is gendered.

In speaking to the gendered history of the profession, the feminization of teaching was largely a result of the expansion of schools during the twentieth century and the need for a cheap, abundant, and well-educated teaching force. White, and generally middle- and upper-middle-class, educated, Christian women, oftentimes excluded from other professions, filled this gap. To promote and legitimize women in the role of shaping young minds, teaching was framed in ways that aligned with other mores about the role of women, including the "cult of domesticity," which saw women as natural nurturers of children.[21] Over time, teaching came to be understood as an extension of these duties with teachers being framed as nurturers of children's minds.[22]

Given the traditionally female teaching force—a reality that persists today (in 2017, 76 percent of all teachers, 89 percent of elementary school teachers, and 64 percent of high school teachers were women and most were White)—the profession has taken on the nature of many feminized professions, including low pay and a low regard.[23] Moreover, perceptions and public narratives regarding what it means to be a good teacher became more situated in building relationships with students, with female teachers often internalizing these views and treating administration as a more technical and thus, male endeavor.[24] Such beliefs were and continue to be reinforced by a predominately male and White administrative force and by external messages through observation and accountability policies that female teachers needed the control and oversight a male expert provides.[25] (One might argue that the modern accountability movement and the inspection of mostly female teachers is an extension of these beliefs.) It is still the case that many female teachers see administration as existing outside the relationship-centered work of teaching and learning and, thus, refrain from becoming administrators or feel a sense of role conflict if they do.[26]

CARE WORK AND EMOTIONAL LABOR

We begin this section by taking a moment to clarify that care or a mothering orientation is neither inherently problematic nor something that should be absent from leadership. Care and relationships are essential to effective leadership and a well-functioning school or school system.[27] Rather, our goal is to provide some context about where the expectation for a particular kind of care comes from, the kinds of bifurcation of roles that developed in education, and how these patterns might keep women from pursuing or accessing leadership roles.

First, notions that women are more naturally suited for teaching than leading can be understood as benevolent sexism in which women are positioned as kinder, more moral, and more vulnerable ("the fairer sex").[28] Like all forms of bias, benevolent sexism is descriptive ("She is such a wonderful teacher, so selfless and caring with her students!") and prescriptive ("She can't possibly live up to the demands of the job and parent two small children. We shouldn't hire her as principal."). In this way, benevolent sexism can limit women's access to leadership given perceptions of both real and imagined maternal demands, an inclination to take care work for granted or see it as in conflict with leadership behavior, and a desire (subconscious or otherwise) to "protect" women from the burden of having to choose between care work at home and leadership. Furthermore, to the extent that women succeed in building effective relationships with their students and their students do well in their classrooms, this success can be used as a kind of performance punishment in that it legitimates arguments suggesting that teachers need to stay in their current teaching roles, even if they desire something very different.

Second, although women's careers are often limited by perceived domestic duties, men's careers generally benefit from having a partner and being seen to engage, even minimally, in the care of their children.[29] Moreover, men often find ways to incorporate their family into their professional life, whereas women show greater reluctance to blur these lines, a factor identified as limiting their access to becoming a high school principal or superintendent for which attendance at various extracurricular activities on nights and weekends is often the norm.[30]

When women are able to access leadership, they are often expected to behave in ways aligned with their "naturally" caring natures. Researchers highlight the ways women must often display care, calmness, and agreeableness and complete additional tasks to keep their workplaces running smoothly regardless of their true feelings or aspirations to do so.[31] Calling this phenomenon emotional labor, researchers highlight how individual emotions become part of the job (e.g., presenting a warm demeanor in the face of a bullying parent or board member).[32] It is perhaps no surprise that women, feeling forced to show emotions that are incompatible with their true feelings, often end up feeling emotionally exhausted and estranged from self.[33] Despite their ubiquity, emotional labor and care work are often invisible in the formal systems and structures of schools and workplaces in general.[34] We might imagine that such invisibility is reinforced through gatekeeping mechanisms to leadership, including hiring and promotion criteria, performance reviews, or merit structures. Indeed, as we discuss in chapter 3, research has shown that although women are expected to present as more caring, doing so can hinder their ability to access leadership roles that they may be ready for and even mar their performance evaluations.

THE DEVALUATION OF CARE: THE STORIES OF FRANCESCA, JOSEPHINE, AND MARIA

Thus far, we have discussed what it means to be socialized in a feminized profession and how care work and emotional labor are both expected of women in schools and devalued. In this section, we transition to stories of women in the field and the ways these elements (feminization and the devaluation of care and emotional labor) play out in women's trajectories toward and success in education leadership roles. These women include Francesca Romano, a teacher working to improve her school and gain access to a formal leadership position; Josephine (Jo) Kim, an assistant superintendent who is denied a leadership position because of views about her role as a mother; and Maria Brown, who is starting a new principal position while simultaneously experiencing dramatic and positive shifts in her home life.

These cases help us see the subtle and not-so-subtle ways sexism (benevolent or otherwise) shapes women's experiences on the path to education leadership. Each of these women, like so many before them, makes numerous sacrifices to balance the oft-competing roles and expectations of being a "good" mother, daughter, wife, teacher, and leader. They each feel a sense of surprise and disappointment about the devaluation of their contributions and that their positionality as women is shaping their opportunities and people's responses to them. You will likely see a number of issues related to these women's trajectories and choices, but we ask that you focus on the way their experiences are gendered and how ideas of care and "mothering" play a role in their decisions and treatment by others. One way to do so would be to substitute a male counterpart in these stories and imagine how the stories might play out differently as a result.

Each case is followed by discussion questions to further probe your thinking and help you to make meaning and draw connections with the big ideas of this chapter. This can be done individually or in community, and we invite you to read the case or cases that feel most salient and useful to you. After the cases, we provide a short summary highlighting shared themes and conclude with some ideas for further exploration as well as ways to disrupt narratives that devalue care and bolster the work of women in the field.

Francesca

Francesca Romano is a teacher leader working at The International School, a private school in India. The school serves predominately US expatriates working in private sector jobs or for the diplomatic service, as well as a smaller number of wealthier locals who want their children to receive a Western education. Francesca identifies as a White, cisgendered, heterosexual woman and is a first-generation American.

She has been with the school since its founding, working hard to develop the student body and support her novice colleagues in enhancing their skills. Francesca aspires to be a school leader and long believed her efforts would translate into bigger and better opportunities in the future. Recently, however, she has begun to wonder whether in an effort to help everyone else, she has actually limited rather than expanded her opportunities for promotion.

Blowing kisses to Nicholas, her now three-month-old nephew and waving goodbye to her sister, both more than six thousand miles away, Francesca closed her laptop and sighed. It was Saturday morning, and her email inbox was already full of requests for her help and time. The second-grade teacher was asking her to take "a quick look" at her lesson plan. The kindergarten teacher had questions about how to best approach a child's parents about his escalating physical behavior. The team leader for the upper graders wondered if Francesca could help answer questions about the new grading software. Scrolling through and wondering how she could help her colleagues and plan for her own third-grade class between now and Monday morning, another email came in. This time it was from her principal, Sheila Hayman, who was requesting a meeting with Francesca early Monday morning. Clearly, Ms. Hayman had read the email Francesca had sent on Friday in which she had frankly laid out her feelings about her job. Francesca recalled its contents:

> *Ms. Hayman,*
>
> *I am sorry to write this to you so late on a Friday, but I am really struggling. While I love collaborating with my colleagues and feel honored to have been put in the role of K–3 team leader, I don't feel like I can keep up with the demand and fulfill my role as a teacher. Instead of planning for my class the way I would like, I am spending all my time dealing with conflicts among members of the team or helping teachers outside my grade level with a variety of needs. I want to be helpful to you and to the school, but I need help. Is there any way that I could be given some release time? Or perhaps you could create a formal coaching position that I could move into? I know we talked long ago about taking*

an administrative role, maybe now could be that time? Again, I am
sorry I waited so long to send this message, but if things don't change
soon, I am not sure I can stay in this position as I feel like I am not serving
the community or my students to the best of my ability.

Francesca

Feeling apprehensive, Francesca began reading Ms. Hayman's email. But she was soon relieved to see that Ms. Hayman was sympathetic.

Francesca,

I am so sorry to hear that you feel so overwhelmed. You are a treasured
part of our school community. We appreciate all you do and please know
we could not be successful without you! Let's discuss this on Monday,
before school. I am sure we can find a way to make your workload more
manageable, even if that means that some of the new teachers receive a
bit less of your wisdom and support.

Sheila

Feeling bolstered and hopeful that Monday's meeting would provide her with some of the additional support and potentially the compensation she felt she deserved, Francesca went to make another cup of coffee. She had a long weekend of work ahead of her and wanted to make sure she was fully caffeinated to push through the ever-mounting demands she faced.

The International School: Growing pains and possibilities. In some ways, Francesca felt she could not blame Ms. Hayman for her current predicament. After all, Francesca had wanted the school to thrive and had committed to the school's "whatever it takes" orientation when she was hired. This attitude and the hard work that accompanied it was paying off; after five years of work building up the school's reputation, enrollment was booming. Many new families had come to the school, with record numbers of applications this year. Although such increases were wonderful, some of the senior staff sensed that newer parents were being drawn more to the reputation of the school than to its philosophy. As a result, a lot of effort was being expended coaching families about the school's purpose. As one of the veteran staff, Francesca was often pulled into meetings with prospective parents or asked to follow up with families who were questioning policies and practices.

To keep up with the expanding number of students, the school had added new classrooms and teachers each year. Class sizes were also expanded; each classroom had two educators and about twenty elementary students. At the same time, the early elementary-grade teaching team (K–3) had almost doubled, growing from seven to thirteen teachers. As the team's chair, Francesca was tasked with providing orientation and mentoring support for these new teachers. And they needed this support. Although many of these teachers had attended elite colleges, few had prior experience in the classroom or strong pedagogical training.

Francesca to the rescue. As one of the most experienced staff members at the school, Francesca was accustomed to taking on more responsibility than her peers. In her first years at the school, she had led professional development for her colleagues and had worked, at the bequest of the administration, to create a new unit of study for her team that would span the grade levels. Francesca felt grateful to expand her leadership skills and appreciated the opportunity to help shape the curriculum. She was also bolstered by the strength of her teaching team. However, since that time, her closest colleagues had left the school to pursue opportunities in the United States. They had been replaced with more junior teachers who seemed less inclined to "go the extra mile." As the proverbial last woman standing, she felt she had to take on more responsibilities to see the school succeed. The kids needed her, and her colleagues needed her. She could not let them down.

Just in the last year, in addition to her own teaching, she had organized trainings on students' social-emotional growth and parent-teacher conferences. The principal had asked her to formally mentor two new teachers coming into the school, but she was also unofficially mentoring most of the team. Francesca also took care to ensure that all the classrooms ran smoothly, creating schedules for families and placing the classroom supply orders.

Recently, Francesca had started to feel burnt out. Many evenings, instead of relaxing or building relationships outside of school, Francesca found herself talking with colleagues and coaching them on how to deal with students who were having difficulty or with their parents. Often these conversations would end with Francesca committing to do the work herself. While Francesca knew this level of involvement wasn't sustainable, the positive compliments and appreciation from her teammates and principal inspired her to continue. She also believed these experiences could be a stepping-stone to a formal leadership role in the future.

Fraying at the edges. Despite Francesca's best efforts to support the team and the school and to meet her own classroom responsibilities, by December, it felt like things had started to unravel. First, there was a feeling among some of her team members that not everyone was pulling their weight. One team member, Ms. White, was struggling to complete her curriculum work on time and, given the collaborative nature of lesson planning, was slowing the entire team's progress.

At the same time the team seemed to be going through a rough patch, so too did Francesca's classroom. While in previous years she would have everything prepared a few weeks in advance, now Francesca was staying up late each night planning for the next lesson. Adding to her stress, two of her students needed frequent one-to-one support. To be fair, Ms. Hayman had asked Francesca whether, given her prior success and veteran status, she was willing to take these students. "I just know they will be best supported in your class, but I understand if it is just too much for you," Ms. Hayman had said. Feeling touched that Ms. Hayman felt so highly of her skills as an educator, Francesca had agreed to take them on.

Monday's meeting. Rushing to put her materials together for her class, Francesca reflected on how the meeting with Ms. Hayman had gone. During the conversation, the principal had reiterated how grateful and thankful she was to Francesca for all her work, telling her "I don't know what we would do without you." She had also told Francesca the school really didn't have the money to pay her more or to hire, as Francesca suggested, a formal instructional coach. Instead, Ms. Hayman had offered Francesca a new title of "teacher leader." While Francesca appreciated this gesture, she wondered how her colleagues would see this, particularly if it did not include increased authority. Her wonderings turned to concern when she had asked Ms. Hayman if she would speak directly to Ms. White about her general progress and work pace and was told that this was really a team matter that Francesca could handle. In the end, Francesca told Ms. Hayman that she did not want the title and instead would pull back on some of her responsibilities, acknowledging that many team members would likely still consider her the leader of the team and act accordingly. Ms. Hayman said that she would try to make clear that they should look elsewhere for support and promised to pull back on some of her own requests to Francesca as well.

Now, walking into her classroom, Francesca felt conflicted about her decision. Should she have taken the leadership title? Could it have helped her transition into a new role? How could she make clear to others, without a formal entry on her résumé, all the work she did at The International School? She also wondered about her colleagues' reactions to Ms. Hayman's next steps. If Ms. Hayman was going to make it clear to the other teachers that they should look elsewhere for support, what would that mean for her relationships with them? How would she feel about not being the go-to person in the building?

QUESTIONS FOR REFLECTION AND CONVERSATION

- What might Francesca being a single woman have to do with others leaning on her for support?

- How does Francesca's history of supporting her peers and engaging in care work in the organization both help and hinder her ability to move into a leadership role? Why do you think that is?
- How might Ms. Hayman have responded differently to better support Francesca and her trajectory? How might Ms. Hayman act as a sponsor and adviser as well as a formal supervisor?
- If you were Ms. Hayman and had the chance to redo the conversation with Francesca, what might you do or say differently?
- What do your reflections suggest about how you might more effectively support other women along their leadership trajectory? What about your own path forward?

Jo

Josephine "Jo" Kim, a Korean American, cisgendered, heterosexual woman, has worked as the student services coordinator in a midsize district for the past ten years. While she has long aspired to lead a district herself, because of the relatively young age of her children and her husband's hectic work schedule, she has refrained from pursuing this goal. More recently, however, with her children a bit older and her husband's business more stable, she has decided to throw her hat in the ring for a superintendent position in a district about forty minutes from her home in a more affluent bedroom community near a major city. Jo was successful in this pursuit and was offered the position. However, at the last minute, the board chair, an older White woman, called to say that they were retracting the offer.

"Wait, what?" Jo's husband Peter yelled. Jo had waited until the end of dinner to tell him that they didn't need to worry about buying a new car for her commute to her new position. "They retracted the offer," Jo explained, as she started clearing plates. "Claudia, the school board chair, called me and said they were going in a different direction. It looks like I'm not going to be a superintendent after all." Peter raged around the kitchen, alternating between grumbling about calling a lawyer and shouting advice at Jo. "Write to them and tell them that they can't treat you this way!" Jo waited for him to run out of steam, too disappointed to join in his anger. Eventually, he took a more resigned tone. "Just forget about it. Something better will come along, and it makes our lives easier anyway. It was going to be a stretch for everyone." Jo was grateful their twin 12-year-old girls, Julia and Jennifer, were at a sleepover. She didn't want to deal with their confusion or have to explain the change of plans.

Peter hugged her and excused himself to catch up on emails. As she finished up the dishes, she thought about menu planning for the following week. But Jo couldn't stop returning to the conversation that had ruined her chance to be a superintendent.

Work–life balancing act. Just a week ago, Jo was riding high. After years as the director of special services in her local district, the first Asian woman to hold a district leadership position in its history, she had finally grabbed the golden ring—superintendent. It had all felt so exciting and surreal, particularly given all the sacrifices she had made to ensure that the girls' and Peter's paths were on track. Peter, a dentist in town, had started his practice ten years ago, the same year Jo had started working in the district. While Peter put in long hours seeing patients and helping run the office, Jo managed the house and almost everything to do with the girls. She passed up bigger and higher paying jobs over the years, even as many of her friends left the district and as different superintendents, some better than others, came and went.

Her girls had been just two years old when she started her current role. The five-minute drive to the office and the flexibility her prior boss had given her made Peter's longer hours possible. As the girls grew, Jo appreciated that her job often allowed her to pick them up from school and to attend many of their activities and events. Soon they would be heading to high school, and while she knew they would still need her, she finally felt she would have a bit more breathing space to explore her career goals and ambitions.

A change in plans. Given her evolving family situation, Jo began to push for that superintendent role she was eyeing. She talked to Peter about it, and they agreed that the girls and his business were doing well and that Peter could spend fewer hours at the office and start helping out more with getting the girls to school and to their ever-expanding list of after-school commitments and social activities. Jo steeled herself to accept a shift in her family role and took a calculated risk. It all seemed to pay off when she was selected as a superintendent.

And now it was all being taken away with one phone call.

The previous Tuesday afternoon, Jo had left her office at 4:30 p.m., rushing to get to the twins' basketball game in a neighboring town. She had just taken her seat in the stands when her phone rang. It was Claudia Brown, her new school board chair and head of the hiring committee. Figuring it was something important but hopefully fast regarding her hiring paperwork, Jo had picked up. "I'm sorry to bother you toward the end of the work day as I am sure you are trying to finish up," said Claudia, "but I had a quick question about the retirement plan that I wanted to run by you."

"Of course," Jo responded. "I actually left the office a little early to see my girls' basketball game so I'm totally available." The conversation continued congenially. Claudia's questions were answered, and Jo thought nothing more about it.

But then on Friday at 5:00 p.m. Claudia called her again, this time with bad news. She told Jo that she had been thinking about their conversation Tuesday night, and how, as a mom with two kids entering high school, "those are years you'll never get back." She told Jo about how much her own children had needed her during the important transition from middle to high school and how grateful she was that she had been able to be at home with them during that time. "I mean, I know you're a working mom already, but I think the time commitment to be a superintendent, even in our little district, would probably be compromised at this stage in your life given that you have two kids. I just don't want to be responsible for you not being there for them or not giving the district what it needs. So we are withdrawing the offer."

Too stunned to respond in any meaningful way, Jo heard herself say, "I'm sorry you feel that way, but I understand. Have a nice weekend."

"You too," said Claudia, "And enjoy those girls. They grow up so fast!"

Jo hung up, struggling to make sense of what had just happened. She remembered that, in keeping with fair hiring practices, during all the hiring meetings and interviews she had had with the board, neither Claudia nor anyone else had ever asked her about her kids, or her husband, for that matter. As a result, she had never mentioned them. She realized now that if she had done so, she might have never made the final round of interviews.

Now, standing in her kitchen, her gloved hands deep in soapy dish water, she shook her head. "Could this really be happening?" she thought. "I just had a high-level position offered to me and taken away because I'm the mom of two teenage girls."

QUESTIONS FOR REFLECTION AND CONVERSATION

- How did benevolent sexism play a role in Jo's offer being revoked? Do you get the sense that Jo identifies this as a driving issue? Why or why not?

- Claudia and presumably the rest of the board seem to have made assumptions about Jo's role in her family and how it would affect her ability to thrive in a leadership position. What do you make of their assumptions? Would such assumptions be made if Jo was a man? Why or why not?

- Have you ever received messages, subtle or explicit, that you should be prioritizing caregiving and family over work? Have you ever given such messages? If you received these messages, how did you respond?

- If you were Jo and had the chance to redo the conversation with Claudia, what might you do or say differently?
- What do your reflections suggest about how you might more effectively support other women along their leadership trajectory? What about your own path forward?

Maria

Maria identifies as a White, cisgendered, heterosexual woman. She and her husband, Paul, an ER nurse, have been married for ten years. After a long battle with infertility, she and Paul decided to foster a baby. Maria has served eight years as a math teacher and seven as a middle school math coach, to great success. As Maria starts a new job as the principal of a science, technology, engineering, and math (STEM) magnet high school, she reflects on her journey to get to this position and some of the triumphs and challenges she faced in doing so.

At 5:00 a.m. on a Monday morning, Maria was putting the final touches on her makeup. "Not too bad for forty-three," she thought. She smiled at herself in the mirror. She was filled with joy. Her first joy was her new family. After all those meetings with lawyers and the Department of Children and Family Services, the beautiful little girl asleep in her crib upstairs would finally legally be theirs. For the past year, Paul and Maria had been foster parents to the now two-and-a-half-year-old Kimberly. Recently, Kimberly's biological mother had agreed to allow Paul and Maria to enter into an open adoption and become Kimberly's legal guardians. Their little family would finally be complete.

Maria's second joy was professional. Today, Maria would get to walk into Washington STEM Magnet High School as its principal. After fifteen years, first working as a math teacher and then as a STEM coach, Maria was finally being given the chance to lead her own building. Even more incredibly, she had been selected by the superintendent to be one of the architects of the school and its mission. Moreover, because it was a magnet school, she had the autonomy to institute many of the innovative practices that she had worked hard to develop in her prior position. It all just felt too good to be true.

Her thoughts were interrupted by the buzzing of her watch with an incoming text. It was Paul letting her know that he was heading to work, he loved her, and he was proud of her. As she went downstairs to prepare Kimberly's lunch and all the other things she needed for her day at preschool, Maria began to reflect on the long road that had brought her to what felt like the biggest day of her career.

A valued member of the community. It was about five years ago, when, after four in vitro fertilization (IVF) attempts and two miscarriages, she and Paul had decided to give up on having a baby biologically. All that money and time gone, and for what? Maria thought her heart would never heal. And yet there were bright spots during those years, too. Her colleagues at Dubois Middle School had been amazing, lifting her up and working to accommodate her many doctor appointments as she juggled her treatments and her responsibilities as the school's STEM coach. There was also a special place in her heart for her principal, Mr. Calloway. Each time she came to him, whether it was to ask for a week of leave to recover from her latest miscarriage or to leave early to see a specialist that had come recommended but was three hours away, he never batted an eye. "You are valued here, Maria. You know I always say health and family first."

Perhaps as a way of working through her disappointment and grief, Maria took the next few years to dig even more deeply into her work supporting teachers and their STEM instruction. She was instrumental in the adoption of a new math and science curriculum and in building its robotics team, now three-time state champions. Maria had worked particularly hard to recruit students to the team who were struggling in their traditional classes or were having behavior issues. The results had been fantastic. Many of these students, feeling more confident and supported, were able to translate their success into classes and interactions with others. Many of the teachers even started calling her the "STEM whisperer," alluding to the calming and positive effect she had on the students. When the local paper ran a story on the team's success, one of her colleagues was quoted as saying, "Maria has done an amazing job turning our 'frequent fliers' into high fliers. She is truly a miracle worker, and I don't know what we or the kids would do without her."

At the same time she was doing all this work at the school, she was also asked to serve on a variety of district-level STEM initiatives and had worked with the superintendent on developing a proposal to the state to build a new STEM magnet high school—the school that she would eventually be tapped to lead.

She began to think about moving into a leadership position. She was feeling strong, successful, and ready to use that certification she had earned all those years ago. She went to her trusted principal, Mr. Calloway, to discuss it.

He questioned her: "Is it really the right time? While you might feel ready to move on, what if you change your mind? I know you and Paul are thinking about adopting, and being a principal with a young child is really hard. I just don't want you to rush into anything and then feel stuck." Maria appreciated his insights and advice. And yet she couldn't help wondering if perhaps it was more for his own benefit than for hers.

A new addition. Her ability to spend time questioning these points, or in fact anything, was disrupted only a few nights later when the phone rang. It was their social worker calling to tell them that a six-month-old girl had just entered the foster system and to ask if they were able to take her in. Without pausing to breathe, both Paul and Maria yelled an emphatic yes. Kimberly arrived that night.

Life over the following years was a whirlwind. Paul, having a more flexible schedule and better leave policies at his job at a private hospital nearby, took some time off to be with Kimberly during the day and eventually shifted his schedule to night shifts on the weekends. Meanwhile, Maria continued to work with the same fervor and passion, finding herself even more invested in the new high school and its success. "I'm worried you're not taking enough time for yourself," her sister, Eliza, said to her one Saturday afternoon as they pushed Kimberly on the swings. "You waited so long for Kimberly to get here, and now you seem to be working even more than when you were trying to get pregnant. Maybe pushing for a leadership position is too much right now. I just don't want you to burn out or get sick."

Maria took in Eliza's words. She didn't want to burn out, and she wanted to be there for Kimberly, but she had waited so long to pursue her dream of school leadership. And now, just when it all felt like it was falling into place, she was being told seemingly by everyone but Paul to slow down and wait. "Am I crazy to think we can do this all?" she asked Paul that evening. "Well, maybe a little," he said, "but Kimberly is doing great, and I can handle it. Don't give up."

Having it all. Feeling emboldened by her conversation with Paul, the next day she approached the superintendent about putting her name in as the founding principal for the new high school. To her relief and surprise, he said, "I was just waiting until you asked. I can't think of anyone better. We need to work through the formalities, but consider the job yours."

Maria could barely contain her excitement, but she was hesitant to share this information with her colleagues or Mr. Calloway until all the documents were signed and the school year had drawn to a close for fear of their response or the opportunity falling through. When she did share the news, the response was hard to take. Some of the teachers cried. Others begged her to stay. But the most alarming response came from Mr. Calloway. Instead of congratulations, she was greeted with anger.

"I can't believe that after all we've done for you that you're leaving us high and dry," he said. When Maria tried to respond, he interrupted. "I am just so disappointed and hurt. We need you, the kids need you, and you're leaving." Maria mumbled an apology and made an excuse about a teacher she needed to observe, quickly leaving the office.

Later, Mr. Calloway apologized and told her that he was happy and proud of her. Yet, any time they were alone together, he would ask her what they could do to make her stay or if she could just stay "one more year to help train up someone else."

It had all been so disappointing and confusing.

Shaking herself back into the present, Maria heard Kimberly stirring on the baby monitor. It was time to start the day and with it, her new life.

QUESTIONS FOR REFLECTION AND CONVERSATION

- How does the frame of benevolent sexism help us understand Mr. Calloway's responses to Maria throughout the case? Do you think Maria experienced these responses as sexist? Why or why not?
- What do you think of the pressure that colleagues and Mr. Calloway put on Maria to remain working with them despite her opportunity to lead a high school of her design? How does such pressure fit with gendered ideas about teaching or leading schools?
- Maria's mentor and sister sent messages that Maria should slow down and not rush into leadership. What do you make of their advice? Would such advice be made if Maria was a man? Why or why not?
- How might Mr. Calloway have better supported Maria's movement from teaching to leadership? If you were him, what might you have recommended?
- What do your reflections suggest about how you might more effectively support other women along their leadership trajectory? What about your own path forward?

MOVING FORWARD

These cases illustrate how care work and benevolent sexism can shape women's access to and success in education leadership. They also highlight the ways stereotyped expectations regarding women's roles in familial life can spill over into the type of supports and opportunities women receive on their path to leadership. We anticipate that these cases may push you to consider other elements of these women's lives, including their relationships with their partners and family members, their decisions regarding their workload, and the timing of various choices. While we encourage robust and open conversations regarding any of the elements of these cases that spoke to you, we hope you will engage directly with the following issues:

- How care work was both expected from the protagonists and taken for granted.
- The ways those around Jo and Maria, and particularly their supervisors, felt the right to comment on and make decisions about what they could handle relative to their familial obligations.
- How colleagues, loved ones, and even the women themselves reinforced and normalized these messages.

In the next section, we offer our interpretations of these issues and then conclude with some resources for how supervisors and those interested in supporting women in the education leadership pipeline may better do so.

UNDERVALUED AND OVERBURDENED

In each case, the protagonist's care work is both expected and taken for granted. This is true for Francesca, who is asked repeatedly by her supervisor and other colleagues to provide support to colleagues and to engage in much of the behind-the-scenes work of running the school. Despite the time and energy this required of Francesca, these requests came without additional compensation or a formal leadership position. This care work also pulled her away from the core elements of her teaching role and infringed on her personal life (she often used evenings and weekends to catch up on her work). We might presume that part of the comfort others felt in requesting help from Francesca was her repeated willingness to take on more as well her status as a single woman, a status that often solicits a devaluing of such women's free time relative to those with spouses and children.[35]

Additionally, because little of Francesca's additional care work was official (she did it to be "a team player"), it's unlikely that she could capture this work on her résumé or leverage it for access to an administrative role. Stories like Francesca's are, in our experience, common and help to explain why it takes women, who often engage in more instructionally focused but nonadministrative roles (instructional coach, teacher mentor, curriculum specialist), far longer to access school and district leadership roles than their male counterparts, despite these women's relevant expertise.[36]

Shifting to Jo, we again see how her care work and others' expectations about her role as a mother shaped her access to leadership. In this case, when Jo simply mentions her children, it triggers Claudia to presume that Jo would want, and perhaps need, to be their primary caregiver. It's taken for granted that Jo will do this care work. Moreover, although one could argue this work is valued in terms of what Ms. Brown perceives a mother should do, it is not valued for the superintendency, Jo's desired role. This perception stands in contrast to treating motherhood as an asset and seeing the skills and knowledge associated with such a role, whatever it might look like, as aligned with and complementing the work of an education leader. Note, too, that Claudia felt emboldened to make this decision on Jo's behalf, illustrating how benevolent sexism can be meted out by women toward one another.[37]

In Maria's case, we see how such sexist tropes can be used to flatter and cajole women into sacrificing their leadership ambitions in favor of "doing it for the kids." When her colleagues and principal learn that Maria is leaving, they pepper her with "compliments" about how much she is needed and how the school and the kids will suffer if she leaves. By framing their comments in terms of Maria turning away from serving students or not caring enough, they draw on deeply held, and often invisible, stereotypes regarding what good women do in society. This orientation is reinforced by Maria's sister and Mr. Calloway when they also send messages that leadership will make her unable to be the type of mother she wishes to be. In such a frame, by leaving her school and pursuing her leadership goals, Maria is breaking the norms of what it means to be a good teacher, mother, and woman.

None of the events in these cases—with perhaps the exception of explicit gender discrimination in Jo's story—should have felt out of step with the everyday work in schools and school systems. In the education field, overwork and care work are normalized.[38] As such, it's perhaps not a surprise that these women have difficulty identifying the discrimination they are facing. Francesca and Jo seem to accept the messages from authority figures saying they are somehow responsible for the trouble they face. For example, when Francesca, speaks to Ms. Hayman, the result is the directive that it's up to Francesca to pull back rather than have the school step up to fairly compensate her for her efforts. Jo seems to internalize her disappointment, naming the reason for her being passed over as being a mother and not the clearly discriminatory actions of the board. In contrast, Maria, perhaps because of the support she receives from her partner, seems less willing to be pushed off the path toward achieving her goals. And yet her decision to hide her new position from her colleagues suggests that she may feel a sense of shame or culpability for her actions.

REWARDING CARE AND SUPPORTING WOMEN'S PATHWAYS TO LEADERSHIP

We note that women who are striving for leadership positions bear some responsibility for obstacles in their paths. As we see in the cases and in research, at times, women need to find support and strategies for better negotiating their share of domestic work.[39] We encourage women to find this support and to engage in domestic work as they wish, and not only as they feel they are expected to. However, there is much that those already in positions of leadership can do to clear these pathways. Because we are experts in education leadership and not family dynamics, this section focuses on ways to create conditions for women to thrive and to challenge discriminatory notions of how they should behave at work or elsewhere.

One way to attend to the devaluation of care work is to begin to value it. Specifically, we can reshape hiring, evaluation, compensation, and promotion structures to incorporate and reward care work. Behavioral economist Iris Bohnet in her book *What Works: Gender Equality by Design* offers several concrete ways to shift these practices to be more equitable and fairer.[40] One example is to create structured interview processes in which all candidates are asked the same questions in the same order, and interviewers don't compare notes until the end of the entire process. It is also important to focus on skills and knowledge and not to project our own values onto others (e.g., as demonstrated in Jo's case, how to best raise children).

Furthermore, we need to ask questions and evaluate candidates based on the requirements of the job, rather than on some other notion of "fit" that is obtuse and possibly, inequitable. The "I know it when I see it" approach to hiring can be highly problematic and is often used across the education leadership pipeline.[41] For more equitable hiring practices to evolve, it is important that the job description and competencies are explicit and available to all who interview.[42]

Although homophily (the idea that likes are attracted to likes) is natural and to be expected, the hiring committee members should do whatever they can to refrain from simply hiring "mini me's" (in the case of education leadership, oftentimes White men or other hiring members who may project their own career decisions and preferences onto the interviewees). Diversity of perspective can benefit a team and needs to be actively managed, even at the micro or individual interviewer level, to guard against inequitable processes. Even using words like "we" in some interviews but not in others can lead to an inequitable process; everyone should feel equally welcome and psychologically safe during the interview process.[43]

To disrupt current practice, it may be useful for those in supervisory positions to engage in trainings or coaching on gender discrimination and how unexamined ways of interacting with female colleagues or employees may be sending unintended messages about their lack of fitness for leadership.[44] An example of this bias might be consistently asking female colleagues about their families and male colleagues about their work. Another might be asking women to be notetakers or to bring food to meetings regardless of their role. While likely intended without malice, such behaviors promote the idea that women are responsible for ensuring comfort and for serving others rather than participating fully as decision-makers. To combat such scenarios, Bohnet suggests a "consider-the-opposite" approach in which individuals are trained to be their own devil's advocate and to come up with reasons why their thinking might be incorrect or, in this case, gender biased.

Language that weaponizes care by using it to pressure women to take on more work or to not move up for fear of hurting the community ("The families and kids need you!") needs to be retired. Audits that capture the more informal care work women are engaging in relative to their official job responsibilities and to one another are essential. Additionally, as Bohnet also points out, it's important to ensure that gendered work is being compensated.[45] In the case of schools, this might mean that that care work is more formally counted as part of the evaluation and promotion process, making teachers, like Francesca, among the first to be considered and encouraged to apply for leadership and administrative posts.

CHAPTER THREE

The Double Bind for Women Leaders

My district supervisor keeps saying I need to be less of a pushover and just demand that the teachers implement the new curriculum as I asked. He just doesn't get that that will be professional suicide. They'll never forgive me for "yelling at them," and I'll kill any of the trust I worked so hard to build.

—MICHELLE (PRINCIPAL)

I just don't get it. Outside of the school, I am a respected and sought-after instructional leader. I literally get paid to share my expertise and to support shifts in practice to standards-based grading. Inside these walls, I might as well as be invisible. Anytime I try to share some of my expertise, I am shot down and told that I should "stay in my lane."

—DANIELLE (TEACHER)

At the same time my team members on the diversity, equity, and inclusion committee look to me for direction and answers, I feel like they don't really want me there. They're like, "Here she goes again, yelling

about justice." Yes, I am driven by social justice and equity, and so
I'm using my position and voice for the kids. You had better believe
I'm going to bring up these issues. I will not be silent. But it also feels
like I am just reinforcing their position that I'm angry and killing any
chance of getting a principal position.

—ANGELA (ASSISTANT PRINCIPAL)

INTRODUCTION

While rewarding and frequently exhilarating, education leadership is
also often frustrating, difficult, and downright exhausting. Such feelings are captured in the research, with studies revealing that the roles
of educational leaders are becoming ever more complex and difficult.[1]
At the same time, researchers argue that moves to make schools more
"accountable," and the implementation of neoliberal policies aimed at
market-driven reforms have produced a kind of "deprofessionalization"
in which educators feel a loss of autonomy and diminished sense of
efficacy.[2] The global COVID-19 pandemic and the ongoing challenges
of racial inequity and other forms of discrimination as well as negative
public narratives about teachers and their motives and capabilities have
only served to exacerbate and more fully illuminate these difficulties.
Recent polls send dire warnings that educators are feeling burnt-out
and questioning how long or even whether they can stay in their roles.[3]

Although these challenges may be nearly universally experienced,
as we talk with women and those from other minoritized groups who
hold, or aspire to hold, education leadership roles, we hear a particular
kind of fatigue that is often overlooked in the general discourse regarding the challenges of the work. Yes, they are tired and stressed for many
of the same reasons as their White male peers.[4] Additionally, they are
stressed because of stereotypical demands related to domestic work and
caregiving made even more intense during the pandemic. (See chapter 2
for more discussion about the intersection of these demands and leadership.) However, the fatigue they tell us about goes beyond these factors.

It stems from meeting every benchmark, responding to criticism with grace, and feeling as though they have to pretzel themselves to achieve seemingly unwinnable expectations about the type of leader and person they should be. It is the fatigue from doing these things and still having the doors to opportunity shut. It is the bone tiredness they feel from constantly working—as one Asian American, female aspiring principal told us—to "be to other people what they need me to be."[5]

We have heard from women that, in practice, such efforts look like not raising their voice, not moving their arms too much, not being too effusive, dressing like a woman but not being too feminine, being tough but not mean, and showing care and compassion but not being soft. Black women in particular have to work hard not to be seen as angry for fear of being discounted or silenced.[6] All of these women feel constantly reminded to be a good teammate, a "good girl," and grateful for the opportunities they are given, while watching with frustration as male peers, most often White, move quickly through the system, rewarded for the very behaviors they feel they are punished for (the so-called glass escalator).[7] These women often feel that education leadership was just not made for them to succeed.

The gut feeling many women have about not being able to "do" leadership "right," in others' eyes, is, in fact, true. But they're not to blame. When given the space and proper support, women thrive in education leadership roles. Indeed, research on female education leaders shows women disproportionately hold many of the most sought-after behaviors and capabilities of effective education leaders (e.g., shared leadership).[8]

We argue that the way education leadership and its associated recruitment, hiring, promotion, and evaluation practices are constructed is the source of many women's limited access to and unease in the role. In this chapter, we present research on role congruity theory,[9] as well as empirical research on women education leaders, to illustrate how current definitions of leadership are steeped in stereotypes that favor maleness (and Whiteness). These stereotypes then serve to shape who is seen as having or not having leadership potential and who can or cannot thrive in leadership roles.

Much of the foundational research regarding role congruity theory, which proposes perceived incongruity between stereotyped female gender roles and leadership roles manifesting in discriminatory attitudes and actions toward female leaders, fails to attend to issues of race or other forms of difference.[10] As such, when most researchers speak to "stereotyped female identities," they are most often discussing White women and their experiences. It is important to acknowledge that stereotypes regarding women of color not only are steeped in gender discrimination but also are racialized and thus different from stereotypes of White women. Research shows that women of color face multiple forms of discrimination related to the intersection of racial and gender identities (i.e., gendered racism).[11] For example, researchers find that Black female leaders receive more neutral responses when they speak up or act assertively (more like the responses White males receive), whereas White women are more likely to face an "agency penalty" (i.e., punishment for acting strong) for doing so.[12] Note that, although we speak to research that identifies women by their ethnic or racial identities, we are aware that these experiences are in no way monolithic for women of color or White women and vary in important ways within and across racial, ethnic, and other forms of differences.

With all that said, research suggests that gender bias is one salient feature of women's experiences in leadership across other kinds of identity, including within and across many racial boundaries.[13] Therefore, role congruity theory can be seen as one, albeit limited, way to begin to understand the role of gender in education leadership.

LEADERSHIP: A SOCIAL CONSTRUCT, NOT A FACT

Before diving into social role theory, we want to clarify what we mean when we say education leadership is a social construct. In the simplest terms, we are saying that our collective understanding of what makes someone a leader is not an objective truth. Rather, it is deeply steeped in other site-specific social systems and structures. For example, in the

United States, as a country with an individualistic culture in which individual success is uplifted over the collective good,[14] it is not a surprise that
characteristics rooted in this worldview (rugged individualism, entrepreneurial behavior, ambition) are generally associated with leadership.
In contrast, many African and Asian cultures are more deeply rooted
in collectivist orientations and tend to elevate behaviors that put the
group's needs before those of the individual.[15] Leadership then, in these
countries, matches this orientation and is often aligned with elements
of "servant leadership"[16] and, specifically, its roots in humility, organizational stewardship, and service.

At the same time that the individualistic culture of the United States
strongly shapes definitions of leadership in our context, research and
experience tells us something quite different about the nature of effective leadership. This is true in education leadership, in which, despite a
wealth of research showing that sharing leadership and trusting teachers
to make effective decisions are key to building continuous improvement,
policies and rhetoric regarding education leadership continue to uplift
a heroic leader who, by force of will, will save the day by demanding
change.[17] As we discuss next, this orientation is problematic not just in
terms of reinforcing ineffective ideas about leadership but also in terms
of shaping women's ability to access and then thrive in such roles. We
begin with a discussion of gender roles and how they shape expectations
of women's behavior in general and as leaders, specifically.

GENDER ROLES

From an early age, we are sent multiple messages from our families, our
schools, the media, and even our religious leaders about how gender is
performed. What does it mean to be a girl? To be a woman? Gender roles
are shared social beliefs about the attributes of women and men; they
are what we might, in daily life, name as gender stereotypes.[18] These stereotypes then shape not only how we think about gender identity (what
a woman looks, acts, and behaves like), but they also become collective

expectations about how those identifying as a particular gender *should* behave. In this way, gender stereotypes are both *descriptive* and *prescriptive* in that they dictate unspoken expectations of feminine and masculine behavior that, when not met, can result in social and even corporeal punishments (such as violence against transgender or nonbinary people).

So what are these expectations? White and Asian women are often described as holding more communal characteristics that center emotion and care.[19] Prescriptively, these women would be expected to be affectionate, nurturing, helpful, and soft.[20] Conversely, men are often described as holding agentic attributes, including being aggressive, dominant, and self-confident. Equally important as we begin to unpack what these stereotyped expectations might mean for women in leadership is that not only are many women understood as and expected to be communal, but they are also perceived as *not* being agentic. The exception, some researchers have argued, are Black women, who are often viewed as too aggressive or dominant. Although, as we discuss, this framing is also binding in that such behaviors are grounded in gendered racism: Black women do not procure the same benefits given to men (White or otherwise) showing similar characteristics.[21]

Again, these are stereotyped views of gender. There are, of course, women who are aggressive and men who are soft and emotional. Indeed, there are all sorts of people across the spectrum from communal to agentic, and this includes those who identify as nonbinary or transgender. With that said, these gender stereotypes persist, as do their rigidity and narrowness in defining the acceptable parameters of behavior for people of all genders. They cause real damage because they do not reflect the multiple and authentic ways that those across gender identities behave and exist, and thus need to be named and attended to.

LEADERSHIP AND MASCULINITY

Having made the case that both leadership and gender are socially constructed, we now shift to putting these constructions in conversation to help us understand many women's experiences in leadership. First, research in the United States has long shown that leadership is often seen as a masculine endeavor, such that the default has long been to "think manager, think male."[22] In study after study, participants of various gender identities name men as being more aligned with leadership qualities and women less so.[23]

This masculine framing extends to education, where the concept of a lone hero—a strong, charismatic, innovative, and ambitious individual meant to come in and save the school or the district—still prevails and aligns with more stereotyped masculine agentic qualities.[24] This alignment of stereotypes helps to explain why men are often cultivated for and fast-tracked to take on education leadership roles, while women are less likely to be seen as "leadership material" and fail to receive similar mentoring support.[25]

ROLE CONGRUITY THEORY

When these two role stereotypes of women as communal and leadership as agentic intersect, it creates role incongruity. Stereotypes regarding leadership roles hold stable, while those exhibiting or perceived to exhibit communal traits (most often women) are deemed unable to meet expectations of the role.[26] As a result, women in leadership, and education leadership specifically, often face a double bind. On the one hand, they can act in ways associated with stereotyped expectations of leadership (i.e., agentic) and thus in conflict with stereotypes of female behavior. On the other hand, they can act in accordance with female stereotypes (i.e., communal) and thus in conflict with stereotyped leadership expectations. The bind is that either choice is associated with negative consequences for access to and success in leadership roles.

For example, when female leaders act in an agentic manner, research tells us that while they may be deemed competent, they are likely to receive negative feedback about their interpersonal capabilities and orientations (being a man-hater, bossy, a bitch), with real repercussions for their ability to move up and thrive.[27] At the same time, men tend not to face such backlash or are even rewarded for engaging in similarly agentic behaviors (boasting, dominance, arguing).[28] As a result, men experience a larger range of permissible behaviors on the road to and in leadership than their female counterparts.[29] For example, in studies looking at gender and hiring practices, when men engage in self-promotion, it increases perceptions of their competence and likelihood of being hired, while having the opposite effect for women.[30]

Alternatively, when female leaders exhibit more communal traits (i.e., more stereotypically female traits), they are often labeled as weak or overly emotional, and thus are not seen as "leadership material."[31] Additionally, as we saw in a group of aspiring turnaround principals we studied, women often get feedback that they need to "tone down" more stereotypical feminine behaviors and communication styles (like moving their hands when speaking or showing emotion) if they want to be "taken seriously" as leaders.[32] Moreover, although it's true that some men receive negative feedback for being overly communal, it's more often the case that they're rewarded for such behaviors, including those associated with parenting.[33] At the same time, as we discussed in chapter 2, women are often expected to engage in more caring and altruistic behavior, including free labor (which, as shown in higher education, makes access to leadership even harder).[34]

As previously mentioned, much of the research on role congruity fails to consider how intersecting identities and particularly race affect the experiences of female leaders of color. Recent work has made clear that the experiences of women from minoritized racial groups are influenced by both their race and their gender.[35] For example, Black women are inversely punished not for their agentic interpersonal orientations but because of deep-seated racist ideas about Black people's competence and ability to lead. Additionally, Black female leaders face a kind of double jeopardy of gender discrimination and racism in which they are scrutinized differently than their White female peers.[36] Latinas, too, often face various forms of discrimination that stem from both their gender and racial identities,[37] and this experience may not be fully captured or captured correctly through role congruity theory.

In practice, research chronicles how women of color receive backlash for engaging in leadership in ways that suggest a clash between stereotypes regarding their gendered and racialized identities and stereotyped male (and White) constructions of the role. For example, in work studying the experiences of a group of Asian American female leaders, the researchers highlighted how "stereotypes of Asian American women, as submissive, quiet, and retiring, work against those who are in leadership positions and deny leadership potential for those who aspire to leadership roles."[38] Additionally, stereotypes about Black women as angry can lead to a pathologizing of their communication style as unprofessional and, with it, a silencing of their voices.[39]

Together then, this work suggests that while incomplete in terms of addressing all the important nuances of women's experience in leadership or the mechanisms that produce them, role congruity theory can provide a window into why so many women in leadership feel a lack of fit and may even leave or opt out of a leadership position as a result. This phenomenon is called second-generation bias and, as scholars Herminia Ibarra, Robin Ely, and Deborah Kolb explain, serves to erect "powerful but subtle and often invisible barriers for women that arise from cultural assumptions and organizational structures, practices, and patterns of interaction that inadvertently benefit men while putting women at a disadvantage."[40]

ROLE INCONGRUITY IN PRACTICE: THE STORIES OF MICHELLE, DANIELLE, AND ANGELA

Having outlined the key elements of role congruity theory and the double bind, we shift now to illustrations of how it shapes female education leaders' work experiences. To do so, we focus on the stories of three female leaders: Michelle Bockman, a new turnaround principal engaging in continuous improvement; Danielle Jordan, a teacher attempting to exert leadership in her school; and Angela Griffin, an assistant principal who wishes to move into the principalship.

These cases illuminate the double bind women experience and the impact it has on how they think about themselves and behave as leaders. Each of these women feels stuck and unsuccessful and gets negative feedback regarding their ability to enact leadership effectively. Although it is possible, and even probable, that these women made missteps and have more to learn, they've also proven their acumen and potential as leaders.

We ask that as you read each story, in addition to focusing on these women's individual orientations and motivations, you keep an eye on alternative explanations for why certain events occur, including stereotypes about gender, race, and leadership. Watch for how the systems and structures of the organizations (such as hiring and evaluation systems, governance, and models of professional development) reinforce or mitigate these stereotypes. These women's supervisors and their actions should be scrutinized and critiqued relative to the concepts and theories previously introduced.

Like the prior chapter, discussion questions following each case provide opportunities to engage in collective, targeted analysis. We invite you to do so with colleagues or to reflect individually. Feel free to just read the case that's most like your current position and interests or read them all, paying attention to differences and similarities. After the final case, we provide a short summary of themes within and across the cases and then discuss some ways to respond to and continue to think about how to address these issues in practice.

Michelle

Michelle Bockman is the principal at Roosevelt Elementary School, a chronically underperforming K–8 school located in an economically depressed manufacturing town outside of a major metropolitan area. Michelle identifies as a White, cisgendered, heterosexual woman. She was the first person in her family to attend college. Her father was part of the district's janitorial staff, and her mother was a nurse's aide at the local hospital. Given her experiences and upbringing, Michelle believes education is the key to opportunity, and she has dedicated her life to serving students.

Michelle is recently divorced and is now a single parent to her fourteen-year-old daughter. Before taking this position, Michelle was a middle school history teacher. After experiencing a string of principals she deemed as "not able to lead themselves out of a wet paper bag," she decided she could do better. When the opportunity to join a free and state-run turnaround principal preparation program presented itself, she jumped at the chance.

At the time of the case, Michelle was concluding her first year as a principal, having been recruited to Roosevelt directly from her preparation program.

Michelle looked at the clock—9:00 p.m. How had it gotten so late? Shutting down her computer marked the end to another long day punctuated with successes (one of her new teachers was making great strides in her higher-level questioning) as well as difficult interactions (her union representative had come to her office yet again just to let her know that "people are not happy" with the agenda for the next professional development session). Walking through the now-empty school, Michelle wondered how long she could go on working so hard and feeling like this. Yes, the school was making progress—student achievement was up, and the culture had improved. But there remained an undercurrent of resistance from faculty to Michelle's leadership and vision, resistance that bled into how her superintendent perceived she was doing in the role. Michelle couldn't understand the negativity that enveloped her leadership; she knew she was deploying best practices and moving the school forward. Why couldn't she catch a break?

She remembered how overjoyed she had been to hear she was hired as the principal of Roosevelt. She told her friends, "It's like a dream. I get to return as the principal to the school that meant so much to me when I was a kid!" Moreover, having recently graduated from a state-run turnaround principal preparation program and seeing many of her classmates, especially women, unable to land positions, she felt extremely fortunate and proud.

She entered her first year with tremendous excitement and decided to follow the guidance of the instructors in her preparation program: start off with a listening tour, talking with teachers, staff, and students and families to better understand the school's challenges and opportunities. It became clear that, despite teachers stating they were using a workshop model, they weren't implementing it fully. Several teachers, many of them newer to the school, revealed a desire for more opportunities to collaborate and share practices. At the same time, they told Michelle that such efforts by the previous principal weren't successful because some of the more senior teachers had pushed back. When Michelle talked to this veteran group, they expressed frustration about the move to a more student-centered model and instead advocated for the principal to do more to intervene with "unruly" students and to respect teachers' ability to run their own classrooms.

Armed with this information, and again in accordance with what she had learned in her preparation program, Michelle took a capacity-building orientation toward the issues; she focused on providing teachers with professional development for reading workshop instruction and new routines, like walk-throughs to support opportunities for greater collaboration and transparency. Although she had experienced some pockets of resistance and, a couple of times in faculty meetings, had had to cut off a teacher who kept pushing back and arguing with her claims about the workshop model ("Prove it!" the teacher repeated as Michelle tried to share the multiple benefits of the model), three months into the job, she was feeling optimistic. She remembered telling her leadership coach, a support provided from her training program, that

> things are moving in the right direction ... conversations are happening. I feel like things that we said we're going to do, we're doing. I feel like I'm able to really engage with people around curriculum and instruction. I'm able to have really thoughtful conversations. I'm

getting a lot of good feedback, despite having to lay down the law with a few of the more vocal "Negative Nancys." Just the other day, a teacher came in and she was like, "I really feel like I need to tell you, you're doing such a good job. Stand your ground. Continue to stand your ground. You're going in the right direction. We need this."

She remembered feeling that sense of hope and promise. When and how had things gone so wrong? Since that early conversation, teacher resistance seemed to only get worse, not better. Word had recently gotten back to her that some of the teachers had been complaining about what seemed to them to be her "soft" touch with students and her inability to make strong decisions. Complaining to a friend after work, Michelle explained, "I think they mock me in my 'let's collaborate,' 'let's talk.' But I don't ever want to give the impression that I'm just willing to shut things down. I believe in collaborative leadership, and I am not going to give that up just because they don't like it!"

Now, almost a full year into her tenure, as she got into her car to go home, she thought maybe she should have listened to her predecessor's advice about how to deal with the teachers from day one. He had told her to watch out for these "real" leaders of the school and to tread lightly: "Just do like me," he said, "I take a 'live-and-let-live' approach, and we get along just fine."

Michelle understood this advice, but she wondered if it was part of the reason the school's performance had failed to improve. Moreover, her superintendent had made it clear that she was hired to "shake things up" and that they wanted a strong, visionary, and innovative leader who would turn the school around. The superintendent reinforced these expectations early in her tenure, when she met with him to get advice about how to deal with some of the pushback she was receiving. He told her, "You're coming across too nice, like you're not going to hurt a fly. You need to push harder. Nobody has ever called them to the carpet before. It's happening, and they don't like it. You've got to remember they don't like it, and they're going to buck it, and they've done it over, and over, and over again. But you need to push through—don't give up, don't be weak."

She took his words seriously, but it seemed like the harder she had pushed, the more pushback she got in return. Even more frustrating was that as the pushback from teachers got worse, her superintendent became less supportive and more critical of Michelle and her capabilities. Most recently, she had heard rumblings that he now saw her as ineffective and unable to keep her building under control. When they interacted, it was usually negative. He would phone her to tell her that she needed to be less of a "pushover" and just demand that the teachers implement the curriculum, and if she tried to reach out, he ignored her calls and emails.

She recently had heard that a group of teachers had engaged in formal grievances with the union. This meant she would have to spend the next few weeks in various mediations. To top it all off, she had just gotten her formal evaluation, and it was more negative than she had expected and included little mention of the positive student outcomes she had achieved. She still couldn't get over one comment from the evaluation: "Teachers say Michelle is aggressive and that she can come off as dismissive or unkind." She was killing herself to be the type of leader her superintendent had wanted her to be and now he was criticizing her for it in the review? Why couldn't she get it right? Maybe, she thought, "I'm just not cut out for this." And yet she still felt committed to the work, to the kids, and to the community. "What should I do?"

QUESTIONS FOR REFLECTION AND CONVERSATION

- How would you analyze the situation Michelle finds herself in? What exactly is the double bind she is feeling? Can you name the "sides" of the tension?
- How do you think the situation might affect her ability to be her best self at work? Why? What makes her feelings of efficacy so important at this point in her career?
- What advice would you give Michelle about next steps? Imagine you're Michelle's good friend. Imagine you're Michelle and really trying to be your own best self coach.

- What do you think would have happened had she followed her predecessor's advice to "live and let live"? Why?
- Imagine you're the superintendent and that you understood the double bind Michelle was facing. What could you do now? What could you have said or done differently to prevent this situation from happening?

Danielle

Danielle Jordan is a high school chemistry teacher in an affluent and predominately White suburb of her state's capital city. Danielle is White, single, and identifies as a cisgender, heterosexual woman.

Danielle has been a teacher at Northeast High School for ten years and is board certified. She takes great pride in her work and is constantly working to improve her craft and to bring in new and innovative teaching practices. She tells people she is a science teacher and uses science to teach. Indeed, Danielle is a prolific author and social media maven, sharing her experiments in pedagogy with people across the globe, and she holds executive-level positions in various teaching associations.

Of the seven teachers in the science department, only three (including Danielle) are women and all are White. Most of the staff at Northeast have been there a long time. Many of the parents are former students who were taught by many of the same teachers. This continuity has helped build a strong sense of tradition and a feeling that such traditions need to be cherished and uplifted. The school has a good reputation for sending its graduates to the honors college at the state university and to elite private institutions, and parents take such outcomes very seriously.

It was natural for Danielle's friend to ask her about the professional development Danielle had facilitated for faculty at her school that afternoon. Danielle had spoken of almost nothing else the past few times she and her friend, Stella, had met up. Danielle had expressed not just her excitement but also nervousness at finally being able to share some of her expertise about standards-based grading with her colleagues.

It wasn't the topic that Danielle was nervous about: she had won many awards from a variety of external professional organizations for her innovative teaching practices, and she had spoken across the country on standards-based grading and had supported other high schools in taking up the model. And yet, in her ten years at Northeast, this was the first formal opportunity she had had to share her new ideas with her colleagues. As she had said to Stella, after one particularly frustrating day before the invitation came, "I just don't get it. Outside of the school, I am a respected and sought-after instructional leader. I literally get paid to share my expertise and support shifts in practice to standards-based grading. Inside these walls, I might as well be invisible. Anytime I try to share some of my expertise, I am shot down and told that I should 'stay in my lane.'"

She hoped the invitation was a sign that this treatment was changing, and she was finally being accepted for her expertise. But her envisioned victory lap had been a disaster. As she told her friend, rather than treat her as an expert, her colleagues had pushed back on every innovative practice she presented. And then there was the culminating ugly incident with Mr. Smith. She shivered, recalling what had happened. "Stella," she told her friend sadly, "it didn't go at all the way I had hoped."

Danielle at school. Danielle, a self-proclaimed "science geek," had, over her ten years at Northeast High School, taught both the general and Advanced Placement (AP) chemistry classes to wide student acclaim. One reason for these positive feelings was her quirky attitude and appearance. She was famous for her science-related puns and for filling her classroom with chemistry-based decorations, including her use of beakers as flower pots and for making each student's desk look like the periodic table of elements.

She was also well-known for her clothes. Petite, with a soft voice, blonde hair, and a curvy figure, Danielle knew she didn't look like a traditional high school teacher. She often got surprised looks when she told people what she did for a living. However, rather than downplay these elements of her appearance, Danielle leaned into them. On a typical school day, you would likely see her walking down the halls in her chosen uniform: high heels, a brightly patterned dress, a lab coat, and bright red lipstick. When asked about her choices by a friend, Danielle made it clear that it was part of her way of being seen in the classroom. "I can't do what they do," she said, speaking about two of her tall, White, male colleagues, "simply walk into classrooms and demand respect. I have to be loud in all aspects to be seen and heard."

Although students had responded positively to Danielle and had treated her with respect, the same could not be said for all of her colleagues. She often found herself interrupted in meetings, or, when she voiced concerns about whether the curriculum was outdated or pressed for the department to incorporate more innovative practices, she was told to "calm down" or that "maybe that works for you, but it won't work in my classroom." She had also received some unpleasant commentary about her appearance. One of her female colleagues, whom Danielle considered a friend, recently suggested that Danielle should do more to "cover up," as she was creating a "distraction" for the boys in her class and making it hard for the other female teachers to be taken seriously.

Through presentations at conferences and participation in numerous honorary societies, Danielle had become a well-respected, if not minor celebrity, science educator. Her Instagram account where she posted teaching tips and conducted chemistry experiments to help illustrate science concepts had fifty thousand followers and growing. She was getting invitations to speak and provide consulting to districts and schools all over the country. And yet she was dissatisfied. What Danielle really wanted was to share her expertise with and to be seen as a leader by her Northeast colleagues. Unfortunately, she was unsure that would happen. However, this all changed when the principal approached her to lead a new initiative to move towards standards-based grading. "Finally!" thought Danielle, "I have a chance to let people see what I can do."

The big day. Twice a month on Wednesdays, students at Northeast left school early so that faculty could be free for professional development. It was such a Wednesday that Danielle finally found herself standing at the front of the cafetorium ready to engage her colleagues in a session on performance-based grading. She wore her favorite red heels for good luck and a smile on her face—a smile that quickly faded as she began to look around the room.

Right in front sat her department chair, Ronald Smith. One of those tall, White men to whom Danielle had compared herself, Mr. Smith had often expressed skepticism regarding standards-based grading (SBG), or, it often seemed, any other ideas that Danielle had brought to their meetings. Today, he had his arms folded in front of him and wore a look that suggested he was ready to fight. Attempting to ignore him, Danielle began by providing an overview of SBG with attention to how it might be implemented across the curriculum. The faculty then split up into groups to discuss an article that proposed eliminating the grades below F (i.e., those below 50 percent) to create more equitable assessment practices.

As Danielle shifted from group work to sharing out, the trouble began. Mr. Smith, flanked by another one of Danielle's male colleagues, said his group disagreed with the premise of the article and that any move to embrace SBG or change a "normal distribution" of grades would lead to less rigor and lower standards in their classes. As Danielle held her ground and began to explain how SBG could serve to increase rigor, Mr. Smith became visibly agitated: "You're twisting my words, Danielle!" he yelled, pointing his finger at her and raising himself out of his chair. When Danielle tried to respond, he began to move toward Danielle, waving his arms and yelling. As he towered over Danielle, yelling that she didn't know what she was talking about and that "it's working just fine as is," her other colleagues looked away, some mumbling to one another or shaking their heads, but none rising to help or intervene. Because these meetings had traditionally been faculty-facilitated, the administrative staff was also absent. With no comfortable way to move forward, Danielle said something about Mr. Smith having "a valid point" and that "perhaps that's enough for today."

Seeming placated by her acquiescence, Mr. Smith turned around, returned to his table, and began to pack up his things to go home. Taking cues from him, her colleagues began to do the same. As the room began to clear, with some folks saying "thanks, Danielle" or "interesting presentation" as they left the room, Danielle remained planted at the front of the room trying to hold it together. Finally, when only a few people remained, she went directly to the women's bathroom, where she sat in a stall until she felt a little better and knew her colleagues had left the building.

The aftermath. Now sitting with Stella, a second glass of chardonnay in hand, Danielle thought about how she could move forward from the experience. All she had wanted to do was bring new and proven ideas to her school. Why would no one listen? One thing she was sure of was that she did not want to expose herself to that kind of criticism or interaction with another colleague again. But, at the same time, she knew she was more of an expert on this topic than many others—a recognized expert at that. So why was it her job to back down? Danielle loved her work, but this really made her question many aspects of the job. She wondered what to do next.

QUESTIONS FOR REFLECTION AND CONVERSATION

- How would you analyze the situation Danielle finds herself in? What exactly is the double bind she is feeling? Can you name the "sides" of the tension?
- How do you think the situation with the meeting might affect her ability to be her best self at work? Why?
- Is there anything you think she could have done differently during the meeting? What would that be? Why do you think your approach might work? Is there anything else she could have changed? Should she have changed her style of dress, for example?

- What advice would you give Danielle about next steps? Do you think this is a safe place for Danielle to teach? To lead? What's the difference?
- Imagine you're an administrator who hears about the meeting later. What would you do and why?

Angela

Angela Griffin identifies as an African American, cisgender woman. She's been married to her husband, Franklin, for twenty-three years. She has two teenage sons, one of whom is about to enter the state university as an engineering student. Her other son is a sophomore in the local high school and on the football team. They live just a few blocks from where Angela grew up. When she was young, the area was mostly inhabited by working-class White people, with a few Black families, like her own. More recently, the area has been going through a period of transition as more families of color and immigrants move in.

While the district has seen some shifts in its student demographics, such changes, because of racialized housing patterns, have been reflected most acutely at the school closest to Angela, Cherry Lane Elementary. Although the student body was shifting, the school staff, so far, had not. Teachers in the school and the district were predominantly White, as was the leadership. Currently, Angela is only one of two administrators of color in the district—the assistant principal (AP) at the high school identifies as Latino—and the only woman of color in such a role.

Angela has been an educator in the district for more than twenty-seven years. She sees her work as a calling and part of her family legacy—her mother, aunt, and sister had all been educators as well. She is a deeply religious woman and finds strength and purpose in her service to her community and its children. She is dedicated to them and to constantly improving herself and her craft as well as being an advocate and role model for her community.

Staring at her inbox, Angela Griffin shook her head in disbelief as she read the email: "We are sorry to inform you . . ." How could this be happening? She had been passed over for a principal position again. While rejection always hurt, the sting this time was too much. "I really thought this time was going to be different." She had served her time as an AP, giving twelve years to three different elementary schools in the district, the most recent being Cherry Lane, where she was the AP and had applied to become the principal.

She also knew she was a team player. When the district asked her to move from her second school to become an AP at Cherry Lane, telling her they needed a "heavy" in the building and someone to whom the students and families of color could "relate," she never complained. She went where she was needed.

Looking around her office at her multiple framed degrees, she knew the hiring committee couldn't have based their decision on a lack of qualifications. Angela had recently earned a doctorate in education, adding it to her master's in English and her certifications as a reading specialist and a special education teacher. She held licenses as a school administrator and for district leadership. Beyond these credentials, Angela had the instructional chops to back them up. Having spent fifteen years teaching English Language Arts (ELA) and producing some of the highest test score gains of any teacher in the district as well as strong student relationships, she was considered an expert teacher by many. During her time teaching, she was awarded the district and state teacher of the year. She knew what she was doing and had the results to prove it.

Just as important to Angela, she had created and maintained loving relationships with her students and their families. She lived near the school and attended a church just a few blocks away. In her years as an educator, she saw many young people flourish and often attended graduations, weddings, baby showers, and other celebratory events of former students. She was proud of and grateful for these relationships and knew what it would mean to them if she, a Black woman from the neighborhood, was appointed principal of Cherry Lane.

And now, after promises from the district, year after year, that she would get to lead a building "as soon as the right fit comes along," it was again not to be. As she learned a few days later, the reasoning was all too familiar, putting salt into her already open wound. "I'm sorry Angela, I tried to push them to hire you," her former principal and now associate superintendent, Cheryl Hurt, told her a few days later, "but they kept getting stuck on you being too forceful in your approach, and how they wanted someone a bit softer and less controversial."

Talking with her sister Shanice, an educator in the abutting district, on the phone later that same evening, Angela vented her frustration. She felt like she was again being punished for the very thing that made her such an effective leader and educator. She told Shanice,

> I have more administrative experience than any of them, even the current principal. I carry that kind of confidence and, yes, the position would be new to me, and I have a lot to learn, but I know this school, I know the families, I know the teachers, I know what needs to happen to make the school better. Yes, I push hard. I ask questions about why things are done like this. When the answer is "Well, we've always done things like this," I'm like, "Well, you do realize that that's not a good enough answer, right? We need to do more than coast to make sure all the students are getting the educational opportunities and outcomes they need to succeed."

Shanice heard how much Angela was hurting and encouraged her to lean on her strength and faith in God and to keep fighting. These words were a balm to Angela and, by the time she hung up with her sister, she felt a bit better. She knew what she was fighting for was worth the arrows slung at her. She was used to it. She had often received critiques like those coming from the hiring committee, particularly as she had long been a vocal change advocate regarding issues of racial and economic justice in the district and beyond.

Angela also knew that leading up to the hiring process, she had put herself out there even more. Specifically, her efforts addressing inequity had only intensified during recent years with the murder of George Floyd and corresponding Black Lives Matter movement as well as the COVID-19 pandemic and its disproportionate impact on people of color.[41] As these issues played out in real time in her community, and, among her students, Angela felt called to action and engaged in multiple activities to ensure her students and families received support. This included fighting to ensure her school was a food distribution site and working with a local company to get hotspots donated to families who needed them. More recently, she was tapped by the superintendent to lead the district's diversity, equity, and inclusion (DEI) efforts. The immediate tasks were to update the ELA curriculum to ensure that students had access to culturally relevant materials and to identify and run trainings for teachers on ways to incorporate antiracist principles into their daily classroom practices.

Through these activities, Angela was viewed as a trusted adviser and advocate for the increasing number of families and students of color. Angela's office was a haven of sorts, often occupied with students or parents needing an ear or a shoulder or simply a place to just be. During the hiring process, many of these families wrote the superintendent to request that Angela be selected.

However, just as her role as a leader in her school and at the district level was growing, so was the subtle and not-so-subtle pushback. For example, in some of the DEI meetings, her colleagues had accused Angela of being "pushy" and said that she was yelling at them. Angela worried her colleagues were presenting her in a negative light to people outside the committee. She knew this would hurt her chances to move up. As she had explained to Shanice previously,

> While the other members of the DEI committee sometimes look to me for direction and answers, I often feel like they don't really want me there. They're like, "Here she goes again, yelling about justice." Yes, I am driven by social justice and equity, and so I'm using my position and voice for the kids. You better believe I'm going to bring these issues up. I will not be silent. But at the same time, it feels like I am just reinforcing their position that I'm angry, and so, am killing any chance of making real change or becoming a principal.

Now her worries had become a reality—the principal job she had yearned for was going to someone from outside the district. The new principal was a young, tall, White man. Angela thought that if that's what they were looking for, she didn't stand a chance. Maybe it was time to take Shanice's advice and leave the district to get a principal job somewhere else. It had worked for Shanice after all. But if she did, who would be there to advocate for her students and their families? Would leaving now be a betrayal of all she stood for?

QUESTIONS FOR REFLECTION AND CONVERSATION

- How would you analyze this situation Angela finds herself in? What exactly was the double bind she was feeling when she was working at Cherry Lane? Can you name the sides of the tension?
- How do you think this context and double bind may have impacted Angela's ability to lead as an assistant principal? Why?
- Is there anything you think Angela might have done differently to not get passed over? What would that be and why might it work?
- Imagine you're Angela's friend. What advice would you give her? Should she leave the school and community? Why or why not?
- Imagine you're the superintendent. Is there anything you wish you or someone else had done differently? You recognize Angela's talents and connection to the community, but you too may have felt you faced a double bind at some point in your career and/or now. How might this recognition impact your own ability to support Angela?

MOVING FORWARD

We hope the cases and the associated discussion questions provide insight into how role incongruity can affect the daily work of women as they attempt to exert education leadership in schools and school systems. While these cases may bring up various issues for reflection and discussion, we're highlighting what we deem to be two key aspects of each case:

- The diminished self-efficacy of the female leaders because of the prejudice they faced.
- The role their supervisors may have played in reinforcing discriminatory behavior.

In addition to reviewing these issues and their relationships to the double binds presented here, we also provide some resources for how to counter this discrimination and move productively forward.

WOMEN'S LEADERSHIP EFFICACY

In each case, the protagonist received mixed and often conflicting messages about how they should engage as leaders, and this left each to wonder about their own efficacy and ability to thrive in their leadership role. For Michelle, such messages came from her teachers, punishing her when she behaved agentically (e.g., challenging her credibility about the workshop model), and when she worked to facilitate more communal orientations toward the work (her perception that they mocked her collaborative approach). Danielle too, received messages that her salient femininity (her physical appearance) made her stand out, but not necessarily as a leader. In contrast, when she tried to take on more agentic qualities and share her expertise with her colleagues, she was treated, at least by her department chair, as a threat who needed to be put in her place. Finally, Angela was encouraged to act communally by attending to the needs of those around her (e.g., being a team player, serving on the DEI committee, providing informal support to children and families of color at the school), but such efforts were not valued in ways that helped her gain access to the principalship. Alternatively, when she acted agentically, asserting her position and commitment to social justice on the DEI committee she was tasked to lead, she was critiqued as "angry" and overly "aggressive" in ways that harken back to the gendered and racist trope of the "angry Black woman," thereby again diminishing her access to a leadership position.[42]

Beyond highlighting how strong, capable women have difficulty gaining access to leadership positions or are harassed, harangued, or otherwise not taken seriously as leaders, these cases also show how such experiences are often internalized. Whether it was Michelle and Angela questioning their leadership acumen and their ability to stay in their organization or Danielle feeling that her exertion of leadership caused a negative reaction, each woman seemed to blame themselves, at least to some degree, for the discrimination they faced. Such internalization of discrimination is a pernicious element of second-degree bias, in that it can cause women to opt out of leadership opportunities or, when they do engage, to do so in ways that reinforce rather than challenge stereotypes.[43] For example, it may move them toward pulling their punches when negotiating to avoid being seen as too pushy, overrelying on technical mastery to demonstrate competence in a highly visible role, or taking up a hypermasculine demeanor to convey a sufficiently leaderlike image.[44] Clearly, strategies that require women to respond directly to discrimination by changing themselves to become more agentic ("leaning in") or communal ("just be nice") are insufficient to truly change women's access to and experiences in leadership at scale.

ANCHORING: FINDING MOORING IN A TURBULENT SEA

Scholars, Ibarra, Ely, and Kolb, offer an alternative to such strategies by suggesting that female leaders need not engage in a continual tug-of-war between being seen as likable or competent. Instead, these researchers argue, women leaders should spend less time considering how others see them and more time "anchoring" themselves in their leadership purpose. As they explain,

> Anchoring in purpose enables women to redirect their attention toward shared goals and to consider who they need to be and what

they need to learn in order to achieve those goals. Instead of defining themselves in relation to gender stereotypes—whether rejecting stereotypically masculine approaches because they feel inauthentic or rejecting stereotypically feminine ones for fear that they convey incompetence—female leaders can focus on behaving in ways that advance the purposes for which they stand.[45]

What does this look like in action? The story of Eugenia Torres is a good illustration. Eugenia, a cisgender Latina, attended the same preparation program as Michelle and was also hired to be a turnaround principal. However, unlike Michelle, Eugenia seemed to spend little time worrying about whether her teachers liked her. Instead, she spent the bulk of her time working to communicate her values and that all decisions, instructional or otherwise, would put kids first. When teachers came to her and complained that she was being unkind or mean to them, she would say, "I'm sorry you feel that I hurt your feelings, and we can talk about that later, but I need to ask you whether you feel that what I am asking you to do is best for kids." Ultimately, the teacher would admit the request was aligned with school values. They also often retreated on their comments regarding Eugenia being mean. When they didn't, Eugenia said she would talk to the teacher about how they could better work together. Over time, these conversations became less frequent, with those unwilling to be held accountable leaving the school. Those who stayed did the work, and the school began to improve in performance and reputation. Moreover, the teachers who stayed became fiercely loyal to the purpose and to Eugenia.

Eugenia's success was hard-fought and required ongoing focus and support to keep her on track and resilient despite setbacks. We argue that for anchoring to be effective, it should include opportunities for leaders to reflect and "try on" their leadership purpose in lower stakes environments, for example, in leadership development and preparation programs. It also requires that women be given the knowledge and tools to recognize how gender bias plays a role in the kind of feedback and opportunities they are given (or not) and the opportunity to talk about their experiences together in safe spaces. Women could also benefit from coaching to help them continue to center their purpose in the face of such discrimination. Although anchoring can be a successful strategy for staying centered in one's work, it doesn't stop discrimination. People will likely still respond negatively to women navigating leadership. Other supports and interventions are needed to more directly address the discrimination they face.

SUPERVISION FOR EQUITY

In the cases of Michelle, Angela, and Danielle, their supervisors seemed to be unaware of the ways they reinforced gender and racial biases in their feedback and interactions.

This was true for Michelle, whose superintendent was constantly telling her to "push harder" and not to be "weak" with her staff. Perhaps, as a White male, he was simply offering advice on an agentic approach that had worked for him. But such advice lacks the perspective necessary to effectively support a leader with a different identity—in this case a woman. Additionally, when Michelle told him that such an approach wouldn't work in her context, rather than listen or try to understand, the superintendent pulled away, suggesting he didn't take Michelle's claims seriously and questioned her approach. The lack of reflection on the intersection of the advice he gave and the elevation of comments saying she was "aggressive" and "unkind" suggest a severe blind spot around these issues.

Angela's supervisors displayed a problematic lack of attention to what her identity and role as the sole Black administrator in her building might mean in terms of the staff's responses to her. Rather than challenge the hiring committee's decision or point to the racialized and gendered nature of their conclusion (that Angela was being "too forceful" and "aggressive"), the associate superintendent simply presented the information as neutral. In so doing, she sent the message that the committee's decision was appropriate and that the problem lay in Angela's behavior. At the school level, her principal allowed Angela to take on the emotional labor of attending to students and families of color without asking deeper questions about how well the White staff was meeting this constituency's needs, providing Angela additional support, sponsorship, or compensation, or moving to hire more faculty and staff of color. The superintendent or associate superintendent failed to attend the DEI meetings or rightly name the critique Angela received (that she was "pushy" and "yelling" at them) as racialized and gendered.

Danielle, too, received little support from her administration. While perhaps extreme in the moment, Mr. Smith's behavior and other faculty's responses suggest a pattern of normalizing bullying behaviors. It also suggests that the administration was taking a blind eye to such behavior, sending clear messages about who is more or less valued in the community. Given Danielle's clear anxiety, justifiably it seemed, at presenting in front of her peers, why did none of the administrators, or at least the principal who asked her to make this presentation, attend to lend support and potential gravitas?

Together, these cases reinforce the need for supervisors—and, we would argue, all members of the professional school community—to learn about gender bias and gendered racism and their relationship with how leadership is defined and enacted and to be intentional about disrupting patterns of bias. Additionally, as we discuss, supervisors need to understand how gender bias and gendered racism are deeply embedded in the policies, structures, and routines of education leadership specifically. According to Ibarra, Ely, and Kolb, such work is critical as "second-generation bias is embedded in stereotypes and organizational practices that can be hard to detect, but when people are made aware of it, they see possibilities for change."[46] In the case of Angela, such awareness might prompt the district to revise hiring criteria that deemphasizes a proven track record of success, family voice, credentialing, and experience and that instead problematically elevates affect, perceptions of fitness, and being "softer and less controversial." Similarly, it might lead to reviews of leader promotions and evaluation systems for similar biases, such as those that produced the negative evaluation of Michelle or made it so difficult for Danielle to exert leadership in her building. The next step would be to use behavioral design principles for equity to shift these processes and create, as Iris Bohnet writes, "better and fairer organizations and societies. [Behavioral design] will not solve all our gender- [or race-] related problems, but it will move the needle, and often at shockingly low cost and high speed."[47]

Eagly and Karau explain:

> Over time, such efforts may also move those in power to shift the actual content of leadership roles and with them, potentially how they are understood and defined.
>
> If these roles were to evolve in a direction requiring more of the communal characteristics typically ascribed to women and fewer of the agentic characteristics typically ascribed to men, the existing female gender role would become more congruent with leader roles, and female leaders should experience decreased prejudice and increased acknowledgment of their effectiveness.[48]

We hope that you will take up some of these ideas and actions in your organizations and work to create the equitable opportunities and outcomes female leaders and your schools and school systems deserve. Just as men are often praised for their ability to have range in their leadership style and so, be agentic or communal as necessary, so too should women be recognized for such ambidexterity. Supervisors, coworkers, and hiring committees all have a role to play in recognizing that leadership effectiveness never requires one "best" way of leading; those "best" ways are often built upon stereotypical models that require dismantling—to unbind those biased practices and perceptions that have left women bereft of the opportunities they so deserve to lead.

CHAPTER FOUR

Shattering the Glass Ceiling and Landing on a Glass Cliff

Given the district's history of underperformance and turnover, I knew the job would be difficult, but I didn't know the board would be so obstructionist in my efforts.

—Keisha (superintendent)

I just keep telling myself that this is my chance to serve, to prove to everyone that I—that people who look like me, who have similar back-grounds—have what it takes to lead.

—Amara (assistant principal)

I turned this whole school around, even when everyone said it was impossible, and how did they repay me? They decide to shut down my school without even having the decency to tell me that they were planning to do it all along.

—Roberta (principal)

INTRODUCTION

A few years ago, Jennie was speaking to a group of female principals who were enrolled in her university's education doctoral degree program. They were discussing how several Black, female principals had recently been hired in one of the larger school districts in the state. When Jennie asked why they didn't look more enthusiastic about what she thought was good news—the district had historically had few women and women of color in leadership positions—the women pointed to the fact that every one of these women had been hired to lead a chronically underperforming and underresourced school. "They only call us when nobody else will say 'yes,'" one of the Black women in the group said, as others nodded their heads. "But what can we do?" she continued. "We love the kids, we have the skills, and we're ready to lead."

The experience these women described—that women and people of color seem to be "given the opportunity" to lead only when an organization is in crisis, underresourced, or otherwise at high risk—is neither unique nor limited to the education sector. This phenomenon is called the "glass cliff," signifying that after women break the proverbial glass ceiling and acquire a leadership position, they often face additional challenges as they attempt to engage in difficult or even hostile organizational environments. In 2005, Michelle K. Ryan and S. Alexander Haslam coined the term "glass cliff" based on their research on the impact of female board chairs on organizational performance for the one hundred performing companies on the London Stock Exchange.[1] Spurred by a newspaper article that suggested that because several companies with female board chairs were in a period of declining revenues, these women had "wreaked havoc" on their organizations, Ryan and Haslam found that, quite contrary to this theory, the few women who were appointed to board chair positions were hired when the company was already in a period of decline. Indeed, it seemed that only when such downturns occurred did these companies open themselves up to hiring a female leader. Additionally, after these women were appointed, their companies share prices tended to increase substantively, although perhaps not to the level before their hiring. Put simply, when women finally got the chance to lead, they did so quite effectively under difficult conditions.

However, rather than being lauded for their efforts or success, Ryan and Haslam, as well as others who have since investigated this phenomenon, find that women often receive fewer accolades than their White, male counterparts.[2] In contrast, when a man is successful in such a difficult role, he is more likely to be given outsized credit as a "savior" as well as other rewards, such as enhanced compensation.[3] Women are also more likely to face greater scrutiny for their decision-making and leadership, receive less support during their tenure, and to be more harshly punished for failure, even when the likelihood of success is quite thin.[4] This differential assessment has real implications for these women's job prospects as well as for other women who might find the door to leadership closing after the current female leader exits.[5] Indeed, when a woman shows less success in leading an organization through a crisis, the tendency is for that organization to revert to their traditional pattern of leadership and to hire a man to replace her.[6]

If this wasn't difficult enough, glass-cliff placements can also simultaneously have a negative impact on a female leader's well-being and reify larger discriminatory ideas about their leadership abilities.[7] As women are placed in more stressful leadership positions, they are also likely to experience negative mental and physical health conditions (e.g., depression, anxiety, high blood pressure).[8] Rather than attribute these conditions to the difficulty of their jobs, however, it is more likely that they will be blamed for a lack of resilience. As Ryan and Haslam explain, "This can be taken as evidence that they [women] are unsuited to leadership positions and, hence, can be 'legitimately' denied opportunities for higher office."[9]

Although much of the early work on the glass cliff was conducted in the corporate arena, the findings have been replicated in other contexts (e.g., academia, politics, school administration, legal profession). Oftentimes, women and people of color are "permitted" to lead only when their respective organization is perceived as being in crisis or failing and when the job has been deemed high risk (being offered a "poisoned chalice").[10] Returning to some of the ideas in chapter 2 about feminization, note that perceptions of organizational crisis are often correlated with leadership roles becoming more open to those traditionally barred from entry (women and people of color). When leadership within an industry becomes more feminized (and presumably more racially diverse), such roles are also characterized as having diminished autonomy, increased workloads, and decreased compensation.[11] In this way, the glass cliff can exist as a negatively reinforcing cycle: the riskier the position, the more likely women and people of color are able to access leadership roles, and the more women and people of color access leadership, the riskier such positions are perceived to be. Leaders, then, are less likely to be seen as successful, given these riskier conditions under which they were hired.

If some of what we describe above sounds eerily familiar to the K–12 leadership context, it should. In recent years, spurred by the accountability movement and accelerated by the pandemic, the work of school leaders has become increasingly demanding, often to the point of being untenable.[12] Relatedly, many have argued the work of leadership has become "deprofessionalized" in that leaders face constant challenges to their autonomy and, with it, their sense of efficacy.[13] While such shifts point to the likelihood that the glass cliff is occurring in the K–12 space, we could find only one study to support this.[14] A lot of adjacent empirical work, however, suggests that it is happening and at scale.

For example, we already know that women of color, in particular, are more likely to be placed in needier and less well-performing schools, relative to their male colleagues.[15] Black women are positioned in such spaces as "clean-up" women, meant to act as change makers under tremendously difficult and undersupported conditions.[16] Moreover, female leaders in such settings often face high levels of scrutiny, criticism, and blame and, as a result, are at a greater risk of failure and with greater consequences.[17] Yet aspiring female leaders may feel compelled to take on such positions because these are often the only opportunities they are offered.

WHAT CAUSES THE GLASS CLIFF?

What factors contribute to women and people of color being preferred as leaders in crisis situations or high-risk organizations?[18] In considering what might be creating these outcomes, some have argued that blatant sexism—and specifically a desire among men to see women suffer and fail in leadership—is to blame.[19] Little evidence supports this view, however. It's more likely driven by more implicit forms of sexism, including in-group favoritism.[20] For example, the clustering of White men in positions of authority in most industries, including schools and school systems, is shown to create a higher likelihood that men will favor male applicants for positions.[21] Men may also subconsciously use their privilege to protect fellow in-group members from taking on riskier positions.[22]

Another hypothesis bandied around is that women are more attracted to crisis or high-risk positions, feeling that they are somehow more able to succeed than their male counterparts under such conditions. Research, however, reveals just the opposite. Men, rather than women, are more likely to be attracted to risky positions and especially when the risk is associated with a lack of social supports.[23] With that said, it may still be more likely for women to say "yes" to glass-cliff positions than men because of a lack of alternatives.[24] As one researcher succinctly explained, "After all, beggars can't be choosers."[25]

Finally, and as alluded to earlier, most scholars identify subtler, although no less pernicious, forms of gender discrimination as driving the glass-cliff phenomenon. For example, in the previous chapter, we wrote about the concept of social role congruity and the idea that leadership is often constructed in ways that uplift stereotypically male, agentic attributes (e.g., ambition, strength, innovation).[26] Women, who are stereotyped as having a more communal orientation (e.g., kind, compassionate, emotional), therefore, are often seen as less capable of or a weaker fit with leadership—that is, if the organization is doing well. When organizational performance is in decline, people tend to seek out leaders with communal traits to address perceived problems.[27] As such, experimental research tells us that when people choose leaders for particular contexts, female stereotyped skills are favored for crisis situations and thus so too may be female leaders ("think crisis, think female").[28]

Some people might be ready to celebrate this uplift of female leaders as those most able to attend to a crisis, but it is important to remember that this elevation stems from stereotypes about who female leaders are or should be.[29] In other words, the shift in perception about what type of leadership is needed in a crisis does not necessarily come from a new or more inclusive view of leadership; limits on women's (and men's) acceptable leadership behavior persists. If anything, the glass cliff simply tells us when people might be willing to temporarily break away from a more masculine stereotyped version of leadership.[30] In this way, we might understand this phenomenon not as just a glass cliff, but also as a "glass cushion" in which White men are consistently given preferential treatment to the least difficult and "cushiest" leadership positions.[31] Increasing the numbers of women and people of color in leadership is important but not sufficient in terms of ending discrimination. What is required is not just equal access in general, but equal access to high-quality leadership roles and opportunities, levels of support and scrutiny, and standards of performance that are applied consistently, across the board.

AFTER A GLASS CEILING, A GLASS CLIFF: THE STORIES OF KEISHA, AMARA, AND ROBERTA

In this section, we share the stories of three female leaders, all women of color, who experienced the glass cliff and its many associated challenges firsthand. We first meet Dr. Keisha Jones, a superintendent of a chronically underperforming urban district, who finds herself, only nineteen months into her contract, being removed by her activist board.

Next, we meet Amara Sok, who has recently agreed to become an assistant principal (AP) under what can only be described as highly difficult circumstances. Finally, we learn about Roberta Johnson, a turnaround principal who, despite a lack of transparency about the true nature of the school's needs and her success in enhancing its performance over her tenure, is abruptly told that her school is slated for closure.

Each of these women had a sense of the difficult circumstances under which they were being asked to lead. We hope these cases illuminate how high levels of skill and personal commitment are not always enough to succeed in a dysfunctional system. Rather than focus on whether these women might have "known better" than take on such difficult positions, we ask that you focus on their motivations for doing so and how their reasoning might relate to their gender and racial identities. For example, what brought them to the point of taking on such a role? Were other options available for them to use their passions, skills, and capabilities? Additionally, we ask you to also pay close attention to whether these women were given adequate and meaningful support to succeed.

In addition to these framing questions, discussion questions follow each case. We invite you to engage in these questions by yourself or in community. Some cases may speak to you more than others; we encourage you to think about the cases that feel most meaningful to you. We also provide a short summary of themes within and across the cases toward the end of this section. We close by considering a path forward and how we might begin to address some of these issues and the discriminatory systems belying them.

Keisha

Dr. Keisha Jones is a lifetime educator who for the past nineteen months has served as the superintendent for Old Forge, a large, urban district. Keisha grew up in Old Forge, attended its schools, and is deeply committed to its children and their families. As one of the only Black, female administrators in the district, she feels the weight of being a role model and recognizes what her success and potential failure, could mean for other opportunities for women.

Keisha identifies as a cisgender, heterosexual woman. She is the first in her family to receive a doctorate.

Switching off the live feed of the district school board meeting on her computer, Keisha shook her head. It was over. Only nineteen months into her three-year contract, and the board had voted, eight to one, to remove her from her position. Maybe she should have listened to all those who had warned her that taking on the superintendency in Old Forge would be a mistake. Yes, she had seen how the previous two superintendents, both White men, had made it only two years before the board had tossed them out. She knew the history of the district, a union stronghold with chronically underperforming schools serving predominately Black and Brown students and a reputation for educators who ignored state and district directives. And yet she had believed that she, a Black woman who had grown up in Old Forge's schools, could do better. She owed it to her community and to all the children in Old Forge who looked like her and deserved more to at least try to turn the schools around. Now, in an instant, all of those dreams had vanished.

It wasn't as if there weren't warning signs from the beginning that this might happen. First, there was the issue of charter schools. As one of the state's lowest performing districts, Old Forge was under accountability pressures to perform and had to implement several reforms mandated by the state, including the creation of charter schools. In addition to pulling away many of the district's talented teachers and administrators, the charter schools had decreased the district's student enrollment numbers and with it their associated per-pupil budget allocations. The district had fallen into an even deeper fiscal crisis with an almost $30 million deficit greeting Keisha at the start of her tenure.

Second, the district was in a protracted labor dispute over the teachers' contract. Teachers, who were, at the time, some of the lowest paid in the state, were demanding substantial raises. The district was refusing and calling for $12 million in personnel cuts to help balance the budget.

Third, the hiring process for her position was fraught and often raucous. The mayor had personally asked Keisha to apply for the position, telling her that she was needed to provide the type of stability the district so desperately needed: "I know it will be an uphill battle, Keisha, but you are a uniter, and we need someone who can attend to the hurt so many are feeling right now."

Many on the board agreed with the mayor. But others disagreed.

These board members, many of whom had backgrounds in business rather than education, had had a different candidate in mind—a corporate financier with three years at the helm of a large charter school network. When advocating for him, they had argued that the district needed someone who was willing to get tough and make hard decisions that others had shied away from. "We need someone with business smarts who understands how to fix the bottom line," a board member argued in one of the closed-door meetings leading up to the hiring decision.

The final five-to-four vote approving Keisha as superintendent made it clear how divided the board was.

The early days. As congratulations from her supporters flooded her email and phone, Keisha couldn't help but worry about what she considered an uphill climb to gain the board's and public's trust. She assured herself that the quality of her work would, in time, win the support of her early detractors and help her succeed in making the changes she felt were so desperately needed in the district. To facilitate this process, Keisha had negotiated a delayed start of four months. She had used this time to engage in a listening tour to get to know the district and its issues and to meet as many educators, students, and families as she could.

Based on what she learned, she decided her first area of focus would be to enhance teacher capacity and practice. She introduced a teacher coaching program in which high-performing teachers already in the district would support new and struggling teachers with their practice. She began to more carefully review the existing teacher evaluation data and patterns of performance year to year and in certain schools. She met with each principal to talk her through their teachers' effectiveness. She worked with them to build more robust evaluation, retention, and, if needed, dismissal processes. Beyond wanting to improve the quality of teaching generally in the district, Keisha thought this approach would help her with the difficult job of cutting personnel. Although this work was hard, as many of the principals and teachers were not used to this level of scrutiny, it was rewarding and, she knew, necessary for success.

Keisha felt she was gaining traction with her initiatives and that, despite a rocky beginning, board relations were moving in the right direction. Part of the reason for this was that the recently elected board president, Douglas Scott, appeared to be a supporter of Keisha's. Douglas touted messages of transparency, accountability, and support for the new superintendent. He called for a new operating culture for the board, one that would foster what he called "collaborative governance."

In a foreshadowing of things to come, however, when Keisha offered some new bylaws that would more explicitly operationalize these stated objectives, Douglas denied her, saying, "Keisha, I told you I am a man of my word. As long as you do what you are supposed to be doing and show some results, I won't get in your way."

Shifting relationships. Douglas's assurances were put to test soon enough when, four months into her post, the board voted to overturn Keisha's decision to terminate a teacher after the teacher had thrown a chair across the room. Saying they had compassion for the teacher, and that, as Douglas put it, "everyone loses their temper now and again," the board sided with the teachers' union and against Keisha and their legal counsel.

At the end of the meeting, Keisha shared that while she was not in a position to change the board's decision, she wanted to go on the record to say she disagreed with it and that she worried about the precedent it set for potential future dismissals. When Keisha approached Douglas after the meeting to see how they might repair and move forward, he briskly told her he was too busy and that he didn't appreciate being challenged in a public forum.

From that point forward, board relations quickly started to deteriorate. First, Douglas began to press for the board to take on a stronger role in the day-to-day work of the superintendent's office (contractual decisions, technical operations, and personnel hires). This included emailing, calling, and dropping in frequently to speak and often argue with Keisha about her decisions and next moves, disrupting her meetings when doing so. When Keisha pushed back on these moves, saying they undermined her authority, Douglas only grew more agitated and began to lash out publicly. As he told the local paper, "I am disappointed with Dr. Jones's unwillingness to make decisions to move the district forward. It is my job as board chair to keep us moving in the right direction and to step in when required."

To reassert some boundaries and decision-making authority, Keisha decided to involve her deputies and other board members as support when dealing with Douglas. The next time he arrived at the district during work hours with a complaint about late school buses, she told him that, moving forward, she would like meetings about policy and procedure to include at least one other board member and a member of her staff. Douglas's response was swift and angry. "What do you mean, you don't want to be alone with me? What kind of unprofessional behavior is this? How can you expect to be taken seriously if you can't even deal with a few questions?" Taken aback, Keisha decided to wait a few days to consider her next steps, thinking Douglas probably just needed a little time to cool off.

She was alerted to how wrong she was when, opening the local paper the next morning, she found an article entitled "Is Dr. Jones Failing Our Kids?" It featured "leaked" quotes from Douglas about his disappointment in her leadership so far and wondering "if she is really up to the job." In addition to feeling embarrassed, she knew these shots would undermine her efforts to gain legitimacy with the principals and the community and hence, her ability to press for change. She had already wasted so much time catering to the needs of the board that she had barely been able to build the type of momentum she had wanted around her initiatives or tout her administration's success.

And there were many things to celebrate. Since taking over, she had worked with the union to end the labor dispute and come up with a contract that both sides could live with. She had found ways to cut some of the budget deficit without mass layoffs. There was even evidence that test scores were improving. But all anyone seemed to notice was the public fight between her and the board.

The ongoing battle for control between Keisha and Douglas finally came to a head the summer when Douglas announced he was running for reelection, with his campaign focusing on promoting greater administrative controls throughout the district. He framed his candidacy as a response to Keisha's efforts and made frequent public statements questioning her fitness for the role and seeding doubts with the other board members. It was these efforts, Keisha was sure, that moved them to vote to remove her.

What now? Still stunned by the board's decision, Keisha began to think about the future.

Her first concerns were about the future of her reform initiatives and how those who had worked so closely with her to implement them would react. But she also wondered about her own next steps. The board, clearly worried about litigation, had agreed to a large severance package—nearly a year of her salary. While some in the media were already decrying the amount as wasteful and unnecessary given current budget constraints, she knew she was going to need it. It was unlikely that any other district of a similar size or with a similarly high profile or substantial budget would hire her, given the nature of her exit.

Her cellphone rang, snapping her back to the present. Looking down she saw it was the education reporter at the *Old Forge Daily*. "So it begins and ends," she sighed as she accepted the call, ready to answer what she knew would be painful questions about the day's events.

QUESTIONS FOR REFLECTION AND CONVERSATION

- To what extent do you think Keisha was a victim of the glass cliff? Explain your reasoning.
- What could or should the board have done to guard against the series of negative exchanges with Keisha? What could Keisha have done differently?
- Have you seen or experienced this kind of scenario in your own work life? What was similar? What was different? What conclusions do you draw?

Amara

Amara Sok is a Cambodian American, cisgendered, heterosexual woman in her mid-thirties. She had been a math teacher in one of her city's most underresourced high schools before enrolling in a state-sponsored principal residency program. She did well in the program and felt excited to put her skills to use as a principal. In particular, she wanted to work in one of her city's turnaround schools serving students like herself. Her family immigrated to the United States when Amara was six years old, and she vividly remembers what it was like to feel so lost at school as well as the kindness of her teachers. Unfortunately, she found the hiring process daunting, particularly given that for much of it she was pregnant with her first child. Unable to gain a principalship, she accepted a position as an AP at a local elementary school.

Settling into the booth at the local diner and ordering her breakfast, Amara thought about what she would tell her friend, Marie, when she arrived. The last few months had been a whirlwind. Beyond the stress of having a new baby had come all the interviews, rejections, and now, finally, a position as an AP at Robinson Elementary School. While she was sure Marie would be excited that she had finally landed an administrative role, Amara also knew that she was likely to ask a bunch of questions about the school and the position that Amara wasn't sure she wanted to answer. She had made a lot of compromises to get this job and just wanted to focus on moving forward. Despite all her training and experience, the offers weren't knocking down her door; it was this job at Robinson or nothing. But Amara was determined to show everyone that she had the skills to make this work, no matter how difficult the assignment might be.

Marie arrived, breaking Amara out of her reverie. Sliding into the other side of the booth, she raised an eyebrow at Amara. "So, tell me everything. Starting with why you took an AP position when you trained to be a principal?"

Amara sighed, shaking her head. Clearly this would not be the simple, celebratory brunch she had envisioned.

After pleading to at least get through her first cup of coffee before the interrogation, Amara began to fill Marie in. She described how tiring it was to go from interview to interview, first while pregnant and then with a newborn at home, only to be told that she just wasn't what they were looking for, never mind that they didn't explain what it was that she was lacking. It was so tiring, in fact, that a month ago Amara had decided to pull back and focus more of her attention on advocating for her community and increasing the representation of Southeast Asians in the leadership ranks at the district. She explained, "I scheduled a meeting with the head of HR and started asking questions: 'Are the hiring practices the same for everyone? If you were audited, would that be the case?' I was asking those questions because I had finally had it. I was like, 'Okay, what is going on?'"

The AP position at Robinson, Amara believed, was a direct result of her pressing the district in this way.

She went on to tell her friend about the details of the job that made it not your typical AP position. First, the school was quite large, almost 1,200 students, K–5. Second, after years of being labeled underperforming, the school was now in turnaround status. This meant that the district had additional flexibility to intervene at the school level and were doing just that. As it had been explained to Amara, rather than keep the school as one entity, they were splitting the school into three, two-grade level academies (K–1, 2–3, 4–5). Additionally, rather than have a single leader overseeing the school, they were hiring three APs, one to lead each academy.

"This is a unique situation," Amara explained. "It's going to be like a three-headed principal. I'm an AP, but I get to make decisions with the other APs in terms of what direction we want the school to go in and how we want to handle things. So, to me, it's not necessarily the title. It's being at the table, being able to push the things that I want to get pushed to change the dynamics of education in the district. So, I agreed to take the position."

"Well, I guess this sounds better than I thought," Marie admitted. "But—and don't get mad at me for saying so—do you really want to start your career at Robinson? It's got quite a reputation."

"I hear you," Amara replied. "But, after all, I trained to be a turn-around leader, and at least I know I am needed and can really help."

Even saying these words aloud, Amara wondered if she really could make the difference she hoped. The school had been plagued by high turn-over, low achievement, and a lack of resources for so long. It had also been through multiple reform initiatives, the academies being only the most recent iteration of these efforts. Moreover, there had never been a Southeast Asian administrator in the school, even though more than 20 percent of the students identified this way. She believed she had to break the cycle and prove that she was the right kind of leader for this, or any, school.

"Last thing about work, I promise," Marie said. "Please tell me that you at least have some good people to work with? To support you?"

"Yes and no," Amara said. She explained how, at the school level, she had "lucked out" with the rest of the AP team. "They know what they're doing. They pretty much ran the school last year. They're very knowledgeable about all the stuff, so I'm just learning, soaking in, asking questions, pushing some thinking. And I already told them, 'Guys, give me a month or two to acclimate myself to the schedule, what's going on, the people. And then, trust me, I will pull my weight.'"

But besides her fellow APs, there were few other sources of support. The secretarial staff, so critical to the work of school leaders, was infamous for their ineptitude. While several prior administrators had tried to move them out of the building, because of their seniority and political connections to the senior leadership of the union (one of the secretaries was the leader's sister-in-law and the other, his cousin), they were considered untouchable. Amara knew she was not going to be able to look to them to learn the ropes. Additionally, the district had made it clear that taking on this role was a sink-or-swim scenario, offering few supports. For example, despite being told that someone at the district office would be named the "acting principal" of the school for administrative purposes (signing off on budget, strategic plan, evaluations), this person had yet to be named—and school was starting in a few short weeks. It was also unclear whether this person would be available to the APs for consultation or support.

This lack of clarity around reporting relationships for the APs and the lack of an acting principal had already caused some issues. For example, when Amara had called her director to find out where she could get last year's attendance records, she was told that there was no documentation available.

"I have no data. Like, none," Amara told Marie. "I'm flying blind here. But I just need to roll with it. It's my last chance to really show them what I can do."

Looking expectantly at Marie, waiting for another round of questions or a disapproving glance, Amara was surprised when she threw her arms around her.

"Don't worry, Amara," Marie said as she squeezed her friend tight. "You're going to be amazing. You've faced these types of challenges before, and you've always come out on top. I have complete faith in you and your talents."

"Thank you, Marie," Amara said. "I appreciate you pushing me to ask these questions and that you always have my back. It's going to be hard, but I know I can do it."

QUESTIONS FOR REFLECTION AND CONVERSATION

- To what extent do you think Amara was a victim of the glass cliff? Explain your reasoning.
- What role do you think "beginnings" play in this case (e.g., taking a "few months," role clarity among her peers, an interim boss, lack of data and support staff)? More generally?
- What do you think about the advice her friend gave? Anything else or different you might have offered to Amara?
- Have you seen or experienced this kind of scenario in your own work life? What was similar? What was different? What conclusions do you draw?

Roberta

Roberta Johnson is a cisgender, heterosexual, Black woman in her late fifties. At the time of the case, Roberta had been the principal of Fredrick Douglass Elementary for two years. Located in Portchester, one of its state's poorest cities, Douglass had been consistently ranked as one of the lowest-performing schools in the state. Roberta began her career as a social worker and before being recruited to become the principal at Douglass, she was a successful turnaround principal in two other schools.

———————

Roberta was still in shock. Two years into her principalship, and two days before the district was to have their big meeting unveiling the strategic plan for the fall, the district leadership told her that her school was slated for closure. How could they be doing this? All of that work for what? They couldn't have had the decency to tell her sooner? Why had they even hired her in the first place? Never before had she felt so set up for failure.

Over the past two years, her team had, under incredibly challenging conditions, worked hard to meet the goals the district and the state had put in front of them. Although it was true that they hadn't met all of them, they had made great progress. Test scores and attendance were up, discipline was down, and teachers were reporting satisfaction levels higher than ever. No one could deny that Douglass had changed for the better. And yet the district had still made the unilateral decision to close the school. Roberta felt a sense of despair.

The path to Douglass. Before coming to Fredrick Douglass Elementary, Roberta had had a long and successful career as a school social worker and then principal. In the two other districts she previously worked in, she had succeeded in turning around the performance trajectory of first an elementary and then a middle school. She had done so by working closely with teachers to build their instructional capacity and socio-emotional skills to ensure that every student was getting the support they needed to thrive. This was grueling work but also very rewarding. And, until now, her leadership approach had been deeply appreciated. As Roberta often explained to those who asked how she had the energy to continually be placed in such difficult assignments,

> I think, in some ways, I'm kind of invigorated by the challenge because I want to change it. I want to be that change agent. You probably could give the people who lead these schools a personality test and you would find that we all have Type A personalities. We're up for the charge, we're up for the challenge, and we're confident in our abilities. I think it's easy for us to take these kinds of opportunities because sometimes it's like, where you got to get your foot in the door and prove yourself.

What she often didn't say, however, was that she didn't know if she had a choice but to take such assignments. As she told one of her closest friends who also happened to be a Black, female principal leading a turnaround school in her former district, "I sometimes wonder if, as a woman of color, I've gotten myself pigeonholed as someone who can clean up these types of schools. I mean, can you imagine them hiring me to lead a magnet school or, God forbid, a suburban school?"

Indeed, in Roberta's experience, few Black women seemed to land leadership roles in her district's highest-performing or best-resourced schools. When she was recruited to lead Fredrick Douglass Elementary, part of her wondered whether taking the job would limit her access to moving up or to other opportunities not in turnaround schools. The other part, and the one that won out, was her sense of faith that she could make a difference. She had done it before, why not at Douglass Elementary?

What Roberta didn't know then but now understood was that Douglass was not like the other turnaround schools she had led—it was in far more dire straits. One of the reasons this was not immediately apparent to Roberta's expert eye was that it had been purposely hidden from her. As one of her teachers eventually told her, the day she had visited for her interview, the classrooms she visited were emptied of any of their so-called problem students. "The district leaders told us how orderly your school was and that we couldn't let you come and see the chaos and confusion here," the teacher said. She also explained to Roberta that teachers were told explicitly not to mention anything negative about the school or its students for fear that they would "scare you away."

However, these directives didn't stop these teachers from asking what Roberta recalled later as somewhat telling questions about the conditions of the school. Specifically, they had asked how she would foresee handling discipline and disruptive behavior. They had also asked about her views on proper reading interventions, curricular materials, and if she thought it was important for a school to have clear teaching standards to which everyone was held. As she told one of her friends in the early months of her tenure when the full dysfunction of the school was starting to come to light, and she was feeling particularly bitter about the deceit, "I think people probably knew if I had too much information, I wouldn't have come."

Problems exposed. Roberta remembered the exact day when she first realized that she may be walking into something other than what she had expected. At the district's year launch meeting, Roberta ran into one of her former classmates from her principal preparation program, Shirley Cohen. "Roberta? Oh my gosh, what are you doing here?" Shirley exclaimed. "Hi, Shirley!" Roberta responded. "I'm the new principal at Douglass." Roberta was surprised at the shocked look on Shirley's face and her response: "Douglass? Well, you certainly have your work cut out for you!" Shirley's reaction had stuck with her and planted the seeds of doubt that would later be confirmed.

Just three weeks into the school year, Roberta was interrupted in her office by two FBI agents asking for all the school's financial documents. Unbeknownst to Roberta, due to her outsider status, but apparently well-known to the district which had been notified of an investigation, her predecessor had embezzled a large amount of school funds. Much of Roberta's time that first year was dedicated to dealing with the fallout of this crisis.

This was, of course, in addition to what turned out to be significant problems with student discipline and a general lack of teacher capacity and knowledge about effective behavioral management practices. Few teachers seemed to have strong relationships with the students or their families and, in general, held relatively low expectations for student performance. Finally, as per the teachers' questions during her interview, instruction was generally poor, and the school seemed to lack standard curriculum or associated instructional resources. In other words, the place was a mess.

In response, Roberta did what she always did—she went to work. She built teacher leadership teams that served to vet and select appropriate curriculum for each grade level. She enlisted the help of a number of community organizations to provide students with tutoring and social supports. Given her history in social work, she also ran several professional development sessions on building students' social-emotional development and slowly increased her presence in classrooms as well as feedback regarding instruction. The school worked with outside consultants to implement restorative justice circles, and Roberta worked directly with a few teachers who had particularly high behavioral referrals on enhancing their classroom management techniques.

While all this work was yielding results (referrals were down, attendance was up, teachers' instruction was improving), Roberta was exhausted and wondering whether she could continue this way. As she told her therapist when, during their first session, the therapist asked what had brought Roberta in: "I am just so weary. Sometimes I just don't want to do my job anymore. I feel like it's taken a toll on me physically. I've probably put on at least thirty pounds since when I started there two years ago. I am not taking care of myself. I do not have any type of work–life balance. I need help or I am going to collapse."

"So, what's holding you back from taking more time for yourself?" the therapist asked. "Why are you engaged in such punishing work?" Roberta responded the only way she knew how, by evoking her commitment to her students. She told the doctor, "I have to make that sacrifice because this is bigger than me. It's about being here for the kids, to do what's right for them." And Roberta still believed this to be true. Close her school or not, Roberta knew she and her staff had made a difference to her students and their families. She had fulfilled her commitment. The question was, what would happen next for them? For her?

QUESTIONS FOR REFLECTION AND CONVERSATION

- To what extent do you think Roberta has been a victim of the glass cliff? Explain your reasoning.
- What might Roberta have done differently to mitigate the experience of negative surprises?
- What do you see as the district's role in creating the glass cliff? What advice might you provide the central office about their practices moving forward?
- Have you seen or experienced this kind of scenario in your own work life? What was similar? What was different? What conclusions do you draw?

MOVING FORWARD

Each of our protagonists found themselves on a glass cliff—tasked with leading an organization facing multiple crises with little support from supervisors. Their cases help to illuminate how and why women and people of color may feel boxed into such scenarios and what their associated costs are. As we discuss next, it may be tempting and even fair to lay some of the responsibility on these women and ask how they might have pushed back or done a better job of advocating for themselves at the beginning of their appointments. We ask, though, that you consider the systematic nature of these women's experiences. For example, using the glass-cliff phenomenon and associated research as a guide, would you anticipate that someone with a more traditional leadership identity would face the same degree of scrutiny as these women? Would they have an easier time garnering resources? Would they have had their career trajectory disrupted to the same extent if they were unsuccessful or only partially successful in their roles? Why or why not?

We invite you to engage directly with the following issues:

- How identity is central to explaining why these women were placed in these positions as well as why their respective organizations were considered in crisis.
- The ways these women's commitment to the communities they serve was used by those in power to bring them into and then keep them in glass cliff situations.
- How these women may have felt constrained by either staying or leaving their leadership positions.

In the next section, we give our interpretations of these issues and then conclude with a discussion of how organizations can work to disrupt the glass cliff and its outcomes.

IDENTITY AND THE GLASS CLIFF IN EDUCATION

It is important to name that each of the organizations these women led served predominately students of color and were underresourced and underperforming—an all-too-frequent injustice that requires our attention and action. As those around these women failed to support them, so too did district officials and board members fail the communities they were serving. We want to acknowledge that these realities are part of a larger legacy of institutional racism that consistently provides inequitable opportunities and outcomes to communities of color. While this issue fills books itself, as it should, for our purposes, we want to spotlight the fact that such education organizations are in critical need of excellent leaders and are often considered to be challenging leadership assignments; therefore, those who lead them (like the women in these cases) should anticipate and receive more, rather than less, resource investments.

Though the glass-cliff phenomenon can and does happen to White women as well, it is not a coincidence that Keisha, Amara, and Roberta all identify as women of color and also purposely chose to serve their communities and attend to what Gloria Ladson-Billings has named the "educational debt"—the accumulated inequities that have produced the deficits in outcomes and access to opportunities for students of color and those from other minoritized groups.[32]

Like many Black women in leadership, Keisha and Roberta faced tremendous scrutiny, and even faced what could be described as deliberate sabotage, as they worked to fulfill their responsibilities and improve their organizations.[33] This scrutiny often felt unwarranted or misaligned with their performance, a common occurrence in glass-cliff scenarios in which the leader holds an identity different from that of the traditional pattern of prior leaders (Keisha was the first Black woman to hold the superintendent role in the district). Roberta's case also fits this pattern, as she was set up by the district to act, as many Black female leaders are likewise stereotyped, as a "clean-up" woman and to fix the mess at Douglass Elementary she inherited. Their unilateral decision to close the school after the conclusion of the federal investigation (and hence the end to their potential culpability), and despite improvements thanks to Roberta's tremendous efforts, suggests they were never genuinely invested in the school or Roberta.

A COMMITMENT TWISTED

Although these women's commitment to serve their communities is laudable, it was exploited by those in power. This was true in Roberta's case, in which she was purposefully left in the dark about the true nature of the challenges at Douglass Elementary, the assumption being, perhaps, that she would feel unable to turn her back on the community once she committed to being the principal. Similarly, Amara's description of her position suggests the district had neither the resources nor the inclination to invest appropriately in the school or her success, instead placing the burden on her to find a way to succeed. When we couple this reality with these women's perceived lack of alternative leadership opportunities, we can understand how their commitment could be used to push them to the edge of the glass cliff, recalling the Black, female principal's lament: "They only call us when nobody else will say 'yes.' But what can we do? We love the kids, we have the skills, and we're ready to lead."

CHOOSING THE GLASS CLIFF?

It's possible to see our protagonists as bearing some responsibility for their situations. It may appear that their commitment to their schools and communities blinded them to the early warning signs. For example, why didn't the tight board vote and subsequent lack of written policy regarding board-superintendent relations give Keisha greater pause? Why didn't she push for clearer work and performance expectations? Similarly, Roberta's interaction with her colleague at the district office shook her, but it didn't push her to take a deeper look at the situation at Fredrick Douglass and its challenges. Amara's concerns about her friend's probing questions suggests that she too had reservations about her ability to thrive at Robinson, and yet she went forward, failing to take steps to change the parameters of the job.

Each of these women could have been savvier in their negotiations and fact-finding, but it's also true that they felt they had few other options to share their leadership skills and knowledge. For Amara and Roberta, this belief was grounded in their lived experiences. Before being appointed as the AP, Amara had spent more than a year trying to find an administrative position in her state to no avail, despite having been trained by the state in an elite principal preparation program. Roberta had built a track record of success in turnaround schools, but this success was double-edged; she had been pigeonholed as a "fixer" and thus, was considered only for difficult placements.

Additionally, these women experienced pressures that made it not so simple to walk away from these scenarios or even to ask for help. As we heard from Keisha, failure in such a setting felt like a career killer. Research tells us this may be true, or at least halting in ways that White men in similar roles may not experience. And asking for help may only serve to reinforce stereotypes about their capabilities or lack thereof.

TURNING THE GLASS CLIFF INTO A SAFE LANDING

In addition to illuminating a discriminatory pattern in the experiences of women and people of color in leadership, the glass-cliff phenomenon shows us why access to leadership is not sufficient to create gender equity in the field. We need to create organizations in which leaders of any and all identities have equal opportunities to thrive. Part of this effort would be to ensure that leaders are given the supports and resources they need to effectively meet the challenges they face. As is true with any effort to create equity, this may mean that some leaders receive more or different supports than their colleagues. For example, we know that women and people of color in education leadership are less likely to receive informal mentorship than their White, male peers.[34] Therefore, it might be necessary to provide formal mentorship for these groups as well as more time to meet during the school day and the resources to do so. This might also mean increasing their budgets to meet some of the challenges they face or doing extra work to connect them with external organizations, decision-makers, and potential sponsors.

Another way to disrupt the glass cliff is for organizations to have clear and objective evaluation criteria for leaders. The looser the performance standards are for leaders, the greater the likelihood that stereotypes and unconscious biases will influence decision-making.[35] These criteria should be set at the beginning of the leader's tenure and in the best-case scenario would be the result of collaboration between her and her direct supervisors. And if there is a place for women to be more proactive, this would be it. Women can build criteria into their formal hiring agreements, clarifying expectations and boundaries for the job before taking it on. This process may also reveal which organizational members can be relied on for support, whether it be career-oriented, psychosocial, or both. Such supports are key to navigating these challenging cliffs.

Our final suggestion is less practical and more of a paradigm change: everyone in the organization must reframe the nature of the problem. In much of the literature and this chapter, the glass cliff is often framed as a problem for women and people of color. What if, instead, we thought of this as a problem for men who are receiving preferential treatment in job assignments?[36] What kind of solutions or interventions might we then introduce? How would we measure progress? For such a reframing, we may want to return to the themes discussed in chapter 3 about social role congruity and our collective tendency to "think leader, think male." More specifically, to attend to the glass cliff, we might have to do some deeper investigations about the lone-hero model of leadership in which stereotypically male (i.e., agentic) characteristics of risk-taking, strength, and strategic thinking are elevated, and the success or failure of an organization is attributable to these individual characteristics. Yes, leadership of this kind is important, but so are the contextual and situational elements shaping the organization that should shape what kind of leadership approach is adopted. Acknowledging this reality can help limit the blame those leading organizations in crisis receive, particularly when many of the issues these leaders faced were set in motion long before they took the helm.[37] Doing so would not just help to challenge the glass cliff, it would also support a more realistic and ultimately effective vision of leadership and organizational improvement.

CHAPTER FIVE

Gendered (Racial) Microaggressions and Death by a Thousand Cuts

I was advocating for a more culturally responsive curriculum and one of the district leaders said, "The students are already reading too many books by Black and Brown authors. That's what's preventing them from being college-ready; the district needs to focus on rigor!" As one of only two Black people in the room and the only one with a literacy background, I was devastated that nobody spoke up to challenge this statement.

—SAMANTHA (HIGH SCHOOL DEPARTMENT CHAIR)

It just feels like there are two sets of rules—one for the old guard, those who were there when the charter started and are mostly White, and then one for the rest of us. God forbid we challenge one of the originals or complain about them. I got the message long ago that when push came to shove, the old guard would always be protected.

—KELLY (DISTRICT INSTRUCTIONAL COACH)

My supervisor told me that my male colleague was going to get the residency I wanted because he had a family to think about, and, as a single woman, I could move more easily. And besides, other districts wanted me and he didn't have other offers. Why am I being punished for being a more viable candidate?

—ELEANOR (ASPIRING SUPERINTENDENT)

INTRODUCTION

When we interview female K–12 education leaders about their experiences, they often say that they have not experienced gender discrimination or gendered racism directly. As we probe further, however, it becomes clear that such experiences are commonplace. For example, women often share stories about colleagues telling sexist "jokes" that diminish their and other female leaders' credibility ("Sheila's acting crazy; she's probably on her monthly"). They report frequent occasions of their authority and leadership acumen being challenged ("Yes, I hear that is your opinion, but what do the real experts say?") and of working in environments that make them feel like an outsider (as the only Latina educator in the building being frequently mistaken for janitorial staff). As these stories were revealed, so too was the pain the women felt and the sense of resignation that such incidents were normal.

Together, these experiences can be understood as microaggressions, which, as defined by Kevin L. Nadal et al., are "brief and commonplace daily verbal, behavioral, or environmental indignities, whether intentional or unintentional, which lie beneath visibility or consciousness and which communicate hostile, derogatory, or negative slights and insults."[1] The power of these incidents to harm lies in their banality and the ability of perpetrators and bystanders to write them off as innocuous, ambiguous, or somehow minor.[2] However, the impact of microaggressions is far from small. They serve to uphold discriminatory systems by reinforcing existing power differentials between groups and can be extremely harmful to the physical and mental well-being of those who experience them.[3] This is true for the many female education leaders who regularly face such slights.[4]

MICROAGGRESSIONS

Although experiences of overt racism, discrimination, and bigotry persist, scholars explain that these and other forms of discrimination often occur in more covert or unconscious forms as microaggressions.[5] These can include nonverbal exchanges (e.g., eye rolling, averted gazes) or as comments directed at the recipient's physical characteristics or behaviors ("How can you be the principal? You look so young!").[6] According to Janice McCabe, microaggressions exist as "subtle and stunning encounters that are a frequent occurrence in the lives of subordinated groups and that impact views of the self."[7]

Microaggressions were initially grounded in the experiences of people of color, but there is growing consensus and research that they are also perpetrated on women, members of the LGBTQI+ community, and those of intersecting marginalized identities.[8] In the following sections, we provide an overview of microaggressions as traditionally conceptualized and then shift to the types of microaggressions women, and cisgendered White women in particular, may experience. Next, using an intersectional perspective, we move to discuss what research tells us about the distinct experiences of Black, Latina, and Asian American cisgendered women and those in education leadership specifically.[9]

RACIAL MICROAGGRESSIONS

Derald Wing Sue and colleagues provide the most well-known taxonomy of racial microaggressions and how they might manifest in situ, which serves as the foundation for understanding other forms of microaggressions perpetrated on those from other marginalized identities.[10] First, microassaults are incidents of overt discrimination manifested in verbal or nonverbal attacks. These actions are most like what people think of

as "traditional" forms of discrimination and are often consciously perpetrated. Microinsults, while sometimes unconscious, often disrespect
a person's identity and can include ascriptions of intelligence based
on identity ("Of course you're good at math—you're Asian!"), treating
individuals as second-class citizens, pathologizing cultural values or
communication ("We're in America, speak English!"), or assuming crim-
inal status.

Microinvalidations, also often unconscious, devalue the recipient and
their identity by treating individuals as foreigners ("But where are you
really from?"), claiming colorblindness ("I don't see color!"), asserting
a myth of meritocracy, and/or denying individual racism ("I don't have
a racist bone in my body!"). These three forms of microaggressions can
occur simultaneously at the individual (micro), organizational (meso),
and environmental or institutional (macro) levels, such that recipients
can experience constant assault or "death by a thousand paper cuts."[11]

A thousand cuts as a metaphor for the impact of microaggressions
is far from hyperbole. Microaggressions produce several serious, negative consequences for those experiencing them, including psychological
distress, depressive symptoms, anxiety, and shame, and their associated
health symptoms.[12] Moreover, given that witnessing harassment can also
produce negative consequences and that there is a heavy cost to coping
with environments in which microaggressions are abundant, we can
understand their impact to be wide-reaching and deep.[13]

GENDERED MICROAGGRESSIONS

Gendered microaggressions are defined as "intentional or unintentional
actions or behaviors that exclude, demean, insult, oppress, or otherwise express hostility or indifference toward women" and exist at the
environmental and interpersonal levels.[14] Indeed, the marginalization
caused by gendered microaggressions can often be attributed less to
individuals and more to deeply engrained organizational structures and
practices that can exclude or diminish women (work retreats that take

place in traditionally male-dominated environments like golf clubs or sporting events). An understanding of gendered microaggressions can facilitate opportunities to investigate whether organizational policies and structures may need to be modified or removed to support a more equitable environment.

Gendered microaggression can occur as follows:

- Gender microassaults (blatant and overt sexist speech or behavior)
- Gender microinsults (unintentional yet sexist statements, "jokes," and behaviors)
- Gender microinvalidations (subtle communication that dismisses or devalues women's thoughts or feelings)[15]

In practice, these microinsults and invalidations can manifest in the form of sexist language and sexual objectification or in treating women as second-class citizens in the organization. This would include paying women less for the same work, a common occurrence in K–12 education leadership (female principals make about $1,000 less than male principals nationally).[16] Gendered microaggressions can also show up as assumptions regarding women's inferiority in particular areas ("women are better at human resources than financial management") as well as in the uplifting of traditional gender roles as applied to the work environment (women always being expected to bring snacks to the meeting or take notes).

More recent work has also identified mansplaining, the phenomenon in which a man, often with less expertise than the women to whom he is speaking, explains something in a condescending or patronizing manner, as a microaggression. This can also manifest as a woman's ideas and suggestions being ignored until a man explains or even simply repeats them, then often taking credit for them.[17] Over time, such patterns can become so normalized that people may not even notice that they have attributed a woman's ideas to a man.[18] Finally, gendered microaggressions can also exist as omissions (failure to act in a gender unbiased way).[19] An example of this would be a leader failing to ask a female colleague to participate on a summer curriculum committee because they assume she would want the summer to spend time with her family, while making no such assumptions about male colleagues.

GENDERED RACIAL MICROAGGRESSIONS

When considering experiences of women in education leadership, it's important to acknowledge that race (among other identities) and the institutional discrimination associated with it creates differences in how women of different racialized identities experience the world. A growing number of researchers are considering microaggressions' intersectional nature and their resultant impact.[20] For example, based on the experiences of Black college women, Jioni A. Lewis and Helen A. Neville developed a widely-used and well-regarded scale on what Lewis named "gendered racial microaggressions."[21] They highlight how long-standing stereotypes (the hypersexual jezebel, the angry and aggressive sapphire, and the strong Black woman) undergird the microaggressions Black women often face.[22] Other identified microaggressions include Black women being silenced and marginalized, being treated as invisible, and being subjected to assumptions about their style and beauty.[23] In practice, such microaggressions manifest in Black female leaders being consistently critiqued for being "angry," told that their hair or appearance is unprofessional, and expected, as discussed in chapter 4, to fix problems in schools that others could not and without proper support.[24]

In our work, we found that Black female aspiring principals face microaggressions in their administrative preparation programs.[25] Among these were being one of few people of color enrolled and a lack of instructors of color (environmental microaggressions). They also reported being tokenized in conversations, particularly when these conversations pertained to race. Finally, we saw a colorblind and "genderblind" approach to teaching leadership that silenced these women and negated the experiences of people of color in leadership more broadly.

Researchers too have identified a constellation of microaggressions unique to Asian American women, grounded in racist and sexist tropes that they are submissive or receptive to sexual advances.[26] Asian Americans and Pacific Islanders (AAPI) in general report experiencing microaggressions based in xenophobia and being viewed as a "perpetual foreigner." AAPI school leaders are often only considered for positions in which they would serve children who were also considered "foreigners."[27]

Without downplaying the rise in anti-Asian hate crimes in recent years, it is also the case that microaggressions lobbed at Asians are often perceived as "positive" and "complementary" by perpetrators ("Your accent is barely noticeable!").[28] Recent work on Asian female education leaders showed they were subjected to microaggressions reflecting the "myth of the model minority," thus invalidating their racialized experiences and essentializing their cultural experiences and identity.

Although perhaps the most nascent in terms of the available research, there is growing interest in and work being done regarding the microaggressions Latinx individuals and Latina education leaders face. These microaggressions are also nativist in orientation, although unique in their allusions to immigration status ("Oh, so everyone in your family is documented?"), communication style ("You're so fiery! Calm down!"), or accents.[29] Racist "jokes" grounded in stereotypes about those of Latinx descent can also be a frequent occurrence, as can the experience of being the one or one of a few Latinx individuals in a space (environmental microaggressions).[30] Like their other colleagues of color, Latina educators are also subject to having these unique racialized (and gendered) experiences invalidated or essentialized as well as experiencing other microaggressions based on stereotypes of Latinas, including when they serve as school leaders.[31]

REPORTING MICROAGGRESSIONS:
A DOUBLE-EDGED SWORD

Given the growing awareness of microaggressions, one may wonder why organizations are not focusing more on these issues and taking action to address them. Again, one of the more insidious features of microaggressions is that they can be difficult to identify and, for those who perpetrate them, difficult to accept.[32] Research tells us that when called out for engaging in a microaggression, perpetrators can respond defensively, denying their comments were intentionally biased ("I didn't mean to offend you!") or suggesting the target is "oversensitive" or "being paranoid."[33] Speaking up can lead to further microaggressions and even negative performance reviews or other professional harm.[34] As a result, it's perhaps not a surprise that those who experience microaggressions tend to quietly shoulder their impact.[35]

LEADING THROUGH A THOUSAND CUTS: SAMANTHA, KELLY, AND ELEANOR

The following set of cases illustrate how gendered and gendered racial microaggressions show up in the daily experiences of three women leaders. The first case focuses on Samantha Brown, a Black woman and high school English department chair serving on a district curriculum committee. Rather than experiencing a welcoming or respectful environment, Samantha finds her views dismissed or ignored and her priority—increasing the representation of Black and Brown authors and diverse characters—denigrated. Next is Kelly Kwan, an Asian American woman who serves as the math instructional coach for a charter school network. Kelly is dealing with a colleague who is harassing and belittling her, an inequitable workload, and supervisors unwilling to intervene on either front. Finally, there is Eleanor, a White woman and aspiring superintendent who is asked to step aside from a choice residency for a male colleague, who, unlike Eleanor, has a partner and two young children.

As per the nature of microaggressions, the degree to which these situations and interactions are gendered, racialized, or both may feel ambiguous to some. Each of these women, however, felt certain that something about them and how they identify shaped their experiences. We ask that you read with an open mind and perhaps a slightly more critical orientation than you're used to. For example, what if, for the purpose of analysis, we accept the premise that gender and racial discrimination is pervasive in our society? What might we see or understand that would not otherwise be available to us?

We also encourage you to pay close attention not only to the interpersonal dynamics in these cases but also to the structures and practices that shape people's experiences within their respective organizations. For example, in the charter network, what might be the relationships between a predominately White leadership team, a teaching staff composed of at least 50 percent teachers of color, and a student body composed of 95 percent students of color? Why is it that in Samantha's and Kelly's cases they are only one of a handful of women of color working in leadership in their districts? How might the recruitment, hiring, and promotion practices of the organization reinforce these patterns? What might that mean in terms of identifying and then addressing environmental microaggressions?

As in previous chapters, discussion questions will follow each case as well as a summary of themes for further exploration. For these cases in particular, we encourage reading across identity lines to explore the intersectional nature of microaggressions and what binds and separates women leaders' experiences. Building on this point, this chapter closes with a discussion of how those with different positionalities relative to microaggressions (target, bystander, ally) can respond to and work to disrupt these events and their institutional underpinnings.

Samantha

Samantha Brown is the English department head at Armstrong High School in the urban center of Highpoint. She identifies as a cisgendered, heterosexual, Black woman. She came to Armstrong eight years ago through the Teach for America program and taught eleventh- and twelfth-grade English as well as Advanced Placement (AP) English. In her fourth year on the job, she was tasked by her principal to develop the English curriculum for her school. Since the implementation of the new curriculum, the school's test scores had improved, and Samantha's class had earned the highest AP pass rate in the city. Thanks to this success, she was first promoted to department chair and then recommended to serve on the district's English and language arts curriculum committee—a task she was initially excited to take part in but that quickly soured.

Samantha Brown felt defeated. After months of sitting through what were often painful meetings at the district office, the curriculum adoption committee for English Language Arts (ELA) had finally made a decision—a decision Samantha vehemently opposed.

Instead of choosing the standards-aligned curriculum that featured authors and stories reflecting the cultural backgrounds of Highpoint's students, district leadership overrode her concerns and selected her least-preferred choice. The official line from the district was that the selected curriculum would be easier for teachers to implement as it was more aligned with "traditional English curricula" and thus more "rigorous." Samantha, however, felt that this decision stemmed primarily from the district leaders' lack of interest in challenging outdated and often White-centered ideas of quality curriculum. She was starting to see that the district's stated commitment to equity was more rhetoric than reality.

It wasn't just their disappointing decision, but also how she had been treated on the committee. Despite being one of few people at the table who had taught English or led an English department, Samantha was often interrupted, talked over, and talked down to. In two instances, the district leaders had started the meeting early before she and the only other school-based person, who also identified as Black, had arrived.

Rather than make a difference on the committee as she had intended, the experience had made her wonder if there was a future for her in Highpoint.

Armstrong High School. In Highpoint, 95 percent of students identify as Black or Latinx and more than 90 percent receive free or reduced-price lunch. Armstrong High School's 1,200 students closely mirrored these demographics. The current superintendent, Fred Burrows, had worked hard to create a sense of urgency around student achievement and results, implementing data teams and other schoolwide instructional reforms to enhance practice across the system and at Armstrong in particular. The district also had a stated goal of enhancing equity; they'd hired consultants to help Armstrong's teachers, 70 percent of whom were White, improve their understanding of implicit bias and culturally competent pedagogy.

Samantha had attended these sessions over the past year and was disappointed, if not surprised, at some of her White colleagues' responses. She remembered one instance in which one of her White colleagues had interrupted the session to say that she didn't understand why they were even talking about these issues. "I treat all of my students all the same, no matter their color!" she exclaimed. The Black teachers, who were all sitting together in the room, had looked to the facilitator to intervene. But silence pervaded the room—until another White colleague turned directly to Samantha and in a loud voice asked, "What do you think Samantha? Do you think implicit bias is operating here at Armstrong?" Taken aback, Samantha responded by talking a bit about her experiences, careful to keep them general and to avoid making eye contact with anyone in particular. "Thank you for sharing, Samantha," the facilitator said. "It is so important to hear *especially* from you." Samantha cringed and left the session feeling even more self-conscious about her status as the only Black leader at the school.

Indeed, while the district had been touting equity, Samantha couldn't help but notice the general lack of people of color in positions of authority. The district office was composed mostly of White, male leaders. Additionally, she was one of the few administrators of color in the district, the only other being Thomas Hines, the assistant principal at the district's technical high school, a Black man who was also tapped for the curriculum committee. The lack of people of color at the top and the centralized nature of the district created a dynamic in which many teachers of color felt that their voices were infrequently solicited in decision-making and that decisions often did not reflect their priorities or their students' needs.

A need for a new curriculum. Recently, most schools in Highpoint were seeing their student results become stagnant or dip, and, except for Armstrong, this was particularly true in ELA. One reason for this downturn was related to the state's raising the difficulty of the state assessment. Another was attributed to declines in student engagement and motivation. Teachers had heard from students and families that they felt the district's curriculum was outdated. They wanted more material that covered current events and that reflected their experiences and histories.

Regardless of its source, declining student achievement was an issue of great worry for the district. A strong charter presence in Highpoint had already lured many students away, and a decline in district performance would undoubtedly lead to further enrollment losses and, with them, decreased funding. It was important that scores improve quickly and one way to do this, district leaders believed, was to adopt a new and better ELA curriculum.

When she first heard that the district was moving to adopt a new ELA curriculum, Samantha was excited. She had already seen how the inclusion of more authors of color and stories featuring those with similar backgrounds and experiences had given students in her class and in other classes where her curriculum had been adopted the boost they needed. Students were coming to class with new enthusiasm and their writing and overall performance was improving. When her principal finally invited her to join the ELA curriculum committee, she knew this would be her chance to share her success and hopefully, to convince others to move in this direction.

Working on the curriculum selection committee. Samantha received an email from the curriculum committee chair, Chris Jones, laying out the scope of the work. There would be six meetings, each following a rigid protocol that included a common rubric to evaluate each proposed curriculum. Looking over the materials, Samantha immediately noticed

QUESTIONS FOR REFLECTION AND CONVERSATION

- To what extent do you think Samantha was a target of microaggressions? Explain your reasoning.
- Are there specific ways the committee was structured, for example its norms, that contributed to Samantha feeling defeated? Alternatively, do you think it was a lack of systems or structures that in some way contributed to Samantha's experiences in these meetings? What might have helped improve the chances of mutually respectful and productive meetings?
- Is there anything that people in those meetings, including Samantha and her supervisors, could have done to change the decision or the way the decision-making unfolded? Why or why not?
- Have you seen or experienced these kinds of scenarios in your own work life? What was similar? What was different? What conclusions do you draw about your workplace as a result?

Kelly

Kelly Kwan serves as the math coach for a charter network with fifteen schools in Titlesburg and its environs. She is one of a group of network content coaches and reports to the assistant superintendent of curriculum and instruction, Ellen Stevens. Kelly identifies as a heterosexual, cisgender woman of East Asian descent. Previously, when she was a school-based math coach, she was one of only three Asian Americans in leadership across all fifteen campuses with no more than one Asian American teacher at each school. Kelly has more than a decade of experience in teaching, curriculum, and instructional leadership across both district and charter schools. Her background also spans elementary, middle, and high school content and coaching. She is the only member of the network coaching team who does not identify as White and is the most recently hired member of the team.

"Another day, another unpleasant run-in with Erica," Kelly thought as she got on her bike to cycle home. Today, Erica Smith, Kelly's professional counterpart in humanities, had been in rare form. In the morning at the coffee station, Erica had asked Kelly why she looked so awful. Overlooking her rudeness, Kelly replied that her appearance was a function of her mental state; she had heard about another anti-Asian attack downtown and was feeling scared and sad.

Erica shrugged. "But nothing happened to *you*, right? I mean, you're safe here. It's not like you're going to get attacked in the office. Bad things happen to people every day in this city. Stop being so dramatic."

Then, right as Kelly was going to respond, Erica's phone buzzed, and she turned and quickly walked to her office.

"I am so sorry that happened to you," said Bill, another colleague who had witnessed the exchange. "I know that Erica has a big meeting today and is feeling stressed. I'm sure she didn't really mean to be unkind."

I disagree, thought Kelly, but she simply smiled at Bill and shrugged.

Working in the network office. Kelly's main role was to provide coaching and support to teachers as they implemented the network's math curriculum. She loved her job and the teachers she worked with. In contrast to her interactions with Erica, the teachers were generally very kind and treated Kelly as a trusted and respected colleague. Sure, there were a few teachers who resisted her support or said things that made her feel uncomfortable. She thought of Terry, a long-serving middle school math teacher who complained that she felt too overwhelmed to change her practice and implement the new suggested math techniques. When Kelly had told Terry that she was more than capable of learning it, Terry had replied, "Easy for you to say. You were born good at it." When Kelly asked her what she meant by that, Terry had mumbled about her not being able to take a complement and shifted to complaining about the new state exam. True too, when Kelly first went to some of the schools in the network, she was often mistaken for a parent liaison or was spoken to as if she might not be fluent in English. But she was so used to these kinds of errors, they barely registered.

What she could not get used to, however, was Erica's behavior. Before working at the network office, Erica had had a long tenure as the principal at one of the network's highest performing elementary schools. While Erica made instructional improvement in humanities a cornerstone of her tenure, she had attended a liberal arts college and majored in American studies. She had neither formal curricular or pedagogical training nor an education degree. All of her experience had come from working up the ranks in the charter network, first as a teacher and then in administration. Additionally, Erica's husband, Jake, taught English at one of the network's high schools and served as an English department chair. Both Erica and Jake had been with the network since its founding and thus, were well-connected throughout the system.

In contrast, Kelly had both an undergraduate and master's degree in education. She was also enrolled in an EdD program at the local university, with a dissertation that focused on supporting teachers' implementation of equity-based math instruction. She had begun her career as a middle school math teacher, worked her way across various grade-level positions, until she finally received a promotion to become the middle school math coach and then, last year, to work in the network office. While Kelly had worked in one of the charter network's elementary schools for three years, compared with others in the office she was a "newbie" and her experience in district schools was often treated as a "blip" rather than an asset. Kelly wondered how much her "outsider status" was a factor in how Erica treated her.

Different rules for different coaches. From the beginning of Kelly's tenure in the network office, her dynamics with Erica could only be characterized as off.

To begin with, Kelly wasn't all that fond of Erica's work ethic. Erica frequently came in late and left early. Teachers Erica coached would call the office looking for her, and Kelly would have to explain that she didn't know where she was.

There also seemed to be differences in the responsibilities for record-keeping between Kelly and Erica. Whenever Kelly logged into the website where coaches were meant to keep track of their visits and notes, she noticed that Erica never had any observations tracked. Erica also didn't use the coaching rubric, despite being required to do so. Kelly did use the rubric, which only made her feel more under the microscope as the newest hire, because all of her data were in the system.

Things only got worse when halfway through the year one of the middle school principals resigned without having completed their evaluations, and their boss asked Kelly and Erica to fill in. Kelly conducted all the math teachers' observations, and humanities teachers who usually worked with Erica. On one occasion, after Kelly gave feedback to a White, male history teacher, she found out the teacher had complained to the associate superintendent about Kelly's affect, saying she was needlessly harsh and didn't seem to really understand the content. Kelly recognized that, being new to her role, she perhaps hadn't built the trust necessary for a productive evaluation experience. But she also felt that the teacher had felt more emboldened to make these claims as a result of her identity as an Asian American woman. As a gut check, she told Erica about it, hoping she might have insights given her relationship with the teacher. Instead, Erica told Kelly "that's just the way he is" and she "better toughen up" or she'd never make it.

The same pattern of her experiences being minimized persisted when Kelly talked to her colleagues about Erica. She was told that Erica had a reputation in the office for being "prickly" and that she "wasn't really a people-person." Such comments, however, were often coupled with excuses about how Erica was facing a lot of personal challenges and that "she doesn't really mean it; she's just stressed."

Kelly's boss, Ellen, was one of the people saying such things. When Kelly tried to bring up her concerns about workload distribution, Ellen defended Erica. "Erica has dedicated her life to this district, as has her husband," she said. "She has years of positive results under her belt showing that her approach works." After this interaction, Kelly noticed that her relationship with Ellen had shifted. Previously, Ellen would meet collectively with Kelly, Erica, and the other coaches to make decisions. Now she often came to Kelly with directives: "Erica and I drafted them during our check-in. I'll send the new policy to you." Kelly came to understand that Erica's behavior was not something that would be attended to or even acknowledged; she was expected to just "get used to it."

Fed up and feeling that she had exhausted normal avenues, Kelly weighed the pros and cons of "going nuclear" and bringing her concerns directly to the superintendent. On the one hand, she thought it was important he know that she felt marginalized and underrecognized based on the quality and quantity of work she produced. On the other hand, she knew doing so could result in retribution or hurt her chances of moving up in the network over time. In the end, and after quickly checking her financials, Kelly decided that no matter the outcome, she needed to speak up, not just for herself but for all those being affected by these discriminatory behaviors. With that thought, Kelly started drafting her email to the superintendent.

QUESTIONS FOR REFLECTION AND CONVERSATION

- To what extent do you think Kelly was a target of microaggressions? Explain your reasoning.
- In what ways do you think the social structure of the organization might have affected the likelihood of these microaggressions? How about the culture of the organization?
- Do you think Kelly should send the email or not? If not, what should Kelly do next, both strategically and tactically? Should she engage with her boss on this topic? If yes, then, how?
- Have you seen or experienced these kinds of scenarios in your own work life? What was similar? What was different? What conclusions do you draw about your organization as a result?

Eleanor

Eleanor Peters, who identifies as a White, cisgendered, heterosexual woman, is finishing up her coursework in a two-year superintendency program at the state university. The program is considered innovative in that it includes a residency model in which students spend months working within a district office on special projects, reporting directly to the superintendent and shadowing them when possible.

Before entering the program, Eleanor was an elementary school teacher for ten years, an instructional coach for the district for five, and a principal at the same elementary where she taught for six more years. She won principal of the year in her state for her innovative approach and partnership work, and her school was named a blue-ribbon school during her tenure. She is board certified and holds an EdD. Eleanor entered the program after finding it difficult to rise in the ranks in her home district, having received the message from the district office that she was needed where she was and from friends on the inside that the superintendent didn't appreciate her constantly outshining his initiatives. Eleanor is both excited and hopeful that she will be placed in a district for her residency where her ideas are fully appreciated and in which she could see herself staying for the long run.

Lingering by the door after class, Eleanor Peters waited until Professor Mary Green had said goodbye to the last of Eleanor's colleagues. It was the final class in her superintendent preparation program; next year, she would enter her residency and work with a coach in small groups. However, instead of feeling a sense of accomplishment or relief, Eleanor was livid.

From the start of the program, Eleanor had done everything she was supposed to and with excellence. She was well-prepared for her classes, contributed just the right amount to show she was prepared and interested but not too much to come across as a know-it-all. She hadn't complained when, during their course on effective communication, she and the other two women in the cohort of fifteen were told "control your faces" and "stop moving your hands so much, it's distracting and no one is going to take you seriously." One of the instructors even commented on Eleanor's clothes (she usually wore pants and a sweater to class), suggesting that she might want to dress a bit more "feminine" to get the hiring committee to warm up to her.

Moreover, as the only unpartnered person in the group and the only female without children, Eleanor had, with good humor, responded to the constant questions about her dating life and about whether she was worried that working so much would keep her from meeting someone. At the same time, Eleanor noticed that when she worked in group projects she was often treated differently than her colleagues because of her "unattached status." Specifically, there was a tendency to presuppose that she had unlimited flexibility and thus could fill in or take extra work over the weekend that her colleagues could not.

As a result of her hard work, and she thought, her decision not to complain about what she felt were problematic aspects of her experience, Eleanor had risen to be one of the program's top students. Most recently, her team's district revisioning plan, a project the program had initiated with a local district regarding improvement efforts, was considered so promising that the superintendent had asked the team to consult with the district to implement it. While thrilled at the opportunity, Eleanor noticed that despite having been introduced as the team lead, the superintendent had directed all of his questions to her two male colleagues, Bill and Richard, and later took Bill's email for the sake of reconnecting.

Later, when the team was celebrating at a bar, Eleanor had let her guard down and asked Bill why he hadn't made it clearer that she had been the team leader or let her answer any of the questions. "God, Eleanor, why do you need to make everything a competition?" he had responded. "He asked a question, and I answered it. Can't you just be happy that we won?"

"Sorry," Eleanor had replied, "I guess you have a point." And yet she couldn't stop wondering afterward whether, if the superintendent left Eleanor off future emails, Bill would make sure she got the information.

Her face reddened with outrage as the sting of recent events came flooding back.

When at last the room was empty, Eleanor approached Mary, with months of pent-up frustration threatening to overflow. Responding to Eleanor's flushed cheeks and angry expression, Mary ushered her to a chair and sat down beside her. "What's happened?" she asked.

Taking a deep breath and steeling herself, Eleanor began her story.

The residency placement. "It all started about a month ago, right after our revisioning presentation," Eleanor began. "The day afterward, Doug called me into his office and told me that, as the program director and given my performance, he was going to give me first pick of residency locations."

"But that's wonderful!" Mary said.

"It would have been, yes," Eleanor said, "but there's more."

Eleanor then went on to explain how, despite this discussion and the program's typical process of sending candidate portfolios to a select group of superintendents throughout the state so they could match their preferred candidate for the following year's residency program, her process had taken a different turn.

"As you know," Eleanor told Mary, "my first choice district was Northpoint, but it looks like it is not going to happen." She then explained how, despite her excellent record and that the superintendent there had reached out to her earlier in the year inviting her to come to the district, Bill was going to be the resident there.

Eleanor was shocked. While program participants usually had multiple districts to choose from, it was also true that some of these positions were more coveted than others. In particular, residencies in the state's few urban centers were more desirable because of their higher pay, scale, and visibility. Having researched the trajectories of program alumni, Eleanor knew those with residencies in places like Northpoint were almost guaranteed to land a position in another urban district of their choice. In contrast, those who took residencies in the smaller suburban or rural districts often struggled to find positions or did so in similarly smaller districts.

Additionally, through her private correspondence with Northpoint's superintendent, Eleanor learned that this was her last year in Northpoint and that she had already informally negotiated to become the superintendent in a large Midwestern city, a city that happened to be where Eleanor grew up and where she eventually wanted to return. Eleanor felt the residency at Northpoint could be an opportunity for her to build a relationship with the superintendent to the point of following her in her transition. As such, working in Northpoint provided a potential opportunity to get her home and thus she was very eager to be placed there.

Doug's news was like a kick in the gut. How could they give it to Bill and not her? Bill, the student who often came to class only sort of prepared yet had felt emboldened to go on about his work as a high school football coach and assistant principal. Bill, who always complained about the program's workload and that he had to stop coaching after missing too many classes. Bill, who always looked a bit disheveled, while Eleanor spent hours every day getting ready.

"I can't believe he got the job!" Eleanor said to Mary.

"Well, what did Doug say?" Mary asked. "Surely, he had some explanation for this decision."

Choosing her words carefully, Eleanor explained how Doug had told her that while she indeed was listed as the preferred candidate for the position in Northpoint, Doug had ultimately decided to match Bill there. As Doug explained it, Bill's family lived in the town next to Northpoint. His kids were enrolled in school there, and Bill didn't want to uproot them.

"He also told me they have another little one on the way, and so the slightly higher pay in Northpoint would make a huge difference to them," said Doug. "And you, Eleanor, don't have those kinds of expenses and are more flexible, so I figured you wouldn't mind being placed in elsewhere."

"But I do mind," Eleanor had stammered. She had explained to Doug how much she wanted to work at Northpoint and why.

To which, Doug had responded, "I'm sorry, Eleanor. I know you're used to pushing your way to the front of the line, but this decision has already been made. You'll have your second choice at Fairview."

When she called her colleague Fred for advice, he too sided with Bill and Doug.

"I get you," Fred had said, "but let's be honest, you'll be fine no matter where you go, and you're more mobile. To be honest, I'm surprised you're making such a big deal about this."

Stung, Eleanor began to wonder whether everyone else was right. Was she somehow acting entitled or selfish?

Her last stop before coming to see Mary was with her adviser, Professor Randy McCain. At first, Randy had seemed sympathetic, agreeing that it seemed like an overstep by Doug to simply choose to place Bill in the position, despite the superintendent's request that it be filled by Eleanor. Encouraged, Eleanor had said, "Yes, I just feel like if I were a man none of this would be happening."

At that, Randy's demeanor shifted. "That is a very serious accusation, Eleanor. And I would disagree. The issue is about opportunities and potential. For example, I happen to know that Bill did not receive other offers while you did and so could be more easily placed elsewhere. I would say that if anyone benefited from their gender, it's you. White men are a dime a dozen in this business. Being a woman is an asset."

Of all her colleagues and advisers, only Mary expressed sympathy. "I am so sorry this is happening," Mary said. "And I wish I had some better advice to give you, but it sounds like you may have exhausted your options. Perhaps the best thing to do is to try to continue your relationship with the superintendent in Northpoint during this residency year and hopefully this will be a bump rather than a full detour from achieving your goals."

Thanking Mary for her time and the advice, Eleanor contemplated her next steps. Yes, she would stay in touch with Northpoint's superintendent, and she would figure out a way, just as she always had done, to reach her goals.

QUESTIONS FOR REFLECTION AND CONVERSATION

- To what extent do you think Eleanor was a victim of microaggressions? Explain your reasoning.
- Think about her meetings with Doug and Fred. Is there anything Eleanor could have said or done differently that might have altered the situation? Why or why not? How about Doug and Fred? What advice would you give them—after hearing Eleanor's reactions?
- What do you think of Mary's advice? Why?
- Have you seen or experienced this kind of scenario in your own work life? What was similar? What was different? What conclusions do you draw about your organization as a result?

MOVING FORWARD

In each case, our protagonist experienced multiple interactions and organizational structures that made them feel like they didn't belong or weren't valued in the space. In response, one option would be to consider each of these events discretely. Doing so, however, might lead us to miss how seemingly small negative interactions are part of a larger pattern of discrimination as well as their cumulative effect on the target. In contrast, a microaggressions framework allows us to see the reinforcing and environmental nature of these experiences as well as their heavy toll. For example, by focusing solely on the problematic way Erica spoke to Kelly, perhaps treating it as an interpersonal issue or one related to civility, it obscures the potentially racialized and gendered nature of these interactions as well as the lack of movement on the part of colleagues or superiors to intervene.

In addition to helping us take a more holistic view of these women's experiences, using microaggressions as a lens facilitates our ability to see how discrimination may be intentional or unintentional. For example, some individuals in these cases seemed to think they were acting from a place of care—for example, the facilitator in Samantha's school asking her to share her experiences or colleagues who told Kelly that Erica was just "prickly." However, rather than provide comfort, these interactions may have perpetrated further harm through tokenization or invalidation. Finally, using the microaggressions framework also provides opportunities for classifying some of these experiences and, in so doing, increasing the potential for directed responses and interventions and/or repair work in these relationships.

ENVIRONMENTAL MICROAGGRESSIONS

These women faced a number of environmental microaggressions, with the lack of representation and affiliation being particularly salient. Each woman was surrounded by few, if any, people of like identities in positions of authority or even among peers. This undoubtedly affected their views on the possibility of their access to and success in leadership. The lack of representation also appeared to influence the degree to which their interests and needs were understood and taken seriously by those in power. Eleanor's interactions with multiple authority figures who denied the gendered nature of her placement decision is just one example of this.

Moreover, for Samantha and Kelly, it is important to note the way the environmental microaggressions they faced were also racialized. Those with the most formal authority and power in their organizations tended to be White and those with the least, students and families, were generally people of color. In both cases, these two women worked in urban areas where schools tend to be underresourced, underperforming, and overcontrolled—a remainder of the institutional racism built into our education system. Similarly, we might understand the limited representation of people of color in the curriculum in Samantha's district as another form of environmental microaggression.

MICROINSULTS

The women also faced multiple microinsults. For example, there was a pathologizing of each woman's communication style. For Eleanor, this became evident in the context of the feedback she and the other women in the superintendent program received that they were too emotive in their communication style ("control your face," "stop talking with your hands"). As we learned in chapter 3 regarding social role theory, such comments are gendered and send messages that something is inappropriate or bad about expressing stereotyped female behaviors in a leadership setting. Samantha's communication was also pathologized, as she was told to "control her tone" when she simply expressed disagreement with a point being made—a comment evoking the stereotype of the angry Black woman who is somehow unable to engage in civil discourse.

Another form of microinsults came through the condescension Samantha received regarding her expertise and intentions to ensure diverse authors and characters. Indeed, despite having a strong track record of success, Samantha's knowledge was dismissed because it didn't align with the White-centered constructions of quality elevated in the committee. Kelly was similarly dismissed by one of the teachers she was coaching. However, in this case and associated with Kelly's Asian identity, the teacher drew from the myth of the model minority and the stereotype that Asians have natural math ability to challenge the efficacy of Kelly's coaching. Kelly was also treated as a foreigner in her own land as it was assumed that she was not a native English speaker or a coach when initially visiting schools to support teachers.

These women also experienced positioning as second-class citizens. For Eleanor this was expressed through sexist ideas elevating Bill's position as a family man above hers as a single woman. Kelly's second-class status came from her heavier workload and expectations without additional compensation or even acknowledgment. Finally, in Samantha's case, the committee's move to begin meetings without the school-based members sent a clear message that they were not considered necessary members of the team.

MICROINVALIDATIONS

In terms of microinvalidations, each of these women faced regular comments that served to deny their gendered and racialized experiences.

For Kelly, this included Erica's comments about Kelly feeling sad and scared because of the attacks on the AAPI community as well as her colleagues' unwillingness to stand up to Erica and their excuses for her behavior. Samantha experienced this same lack of support from others on the committee as well as the suggestion that, unlike the district representatives, her views regarding the curriculum were primarily shaped by her identity. Finally, Eleanor received multiple messages that despite her feelings and experiences, gender was not an issue in her placement (although it clearly was), redirecting the conversation toward critiquing Eleanor's drive and competitive nature.

PUNISHED FOR SPEAKING OUT

Let's highlight what happened when each woman tried to speak up and name the microaggressions they experienced. They were told, whether subtly or explicitly, that they were being oversensitive or, in Eleanor's case, reading the situation wrong. They were also reprimanded or subtly punished for speaking out. For example, after telling her boss about Erica, Kelly appeared to be frozen out of meetings. In Eleanor and Samantha's cases, the punishment came in the form of disapproval from an authority figure. The lack of support or intervention then put the full burden of coping with these microaggressions on the woman experiencing them, a reality that explains Samantha's decision to pull back from speaking in the meetings as a means of protecting herself.

Together, these experiences also highlight and reinforce that it cannot be the role of those most harmed by microaggressions to be the individuals most responsible for responding to and disrupting them. Instead, it is the responsibility of bystanders and allies to make these efforts.

DISRUPTING MICROAGGRESSIONS

Microaggressions can operate at different levels (interpersonal, organizational, and institutional) and engage people in different ways. Specifically, there are those who perpetrate the microaggression (perpetrators), those who experience the microaggression (targets), and those who witness the microaggression (bystanders). In some cases, there are individuals who speak up or intervene directly on behalf of the target (allies). It is important to embolden these latter two groups through ongoing training and support.[36] Indeed, any strategy to disrupt microaggressions needs to simultaneously attend to how they manifest across the organization and each of the participating groups.

Note, however, that the primary burden for disrupting microaggressions should *not* fall on the targets. Too often those most harmed by discrimination are the ones who are tasked, at great personal and professional risk, to speak up and fight it. Instead, it's important that bystanders and allies take collective ownership of responding to microaggressions and do so whenever they occur.

Those traditionally acting as bystanders must be educated and supported to shift toward action. This is particularly true if these bystanders are members of privileged social identity groups, as they are perhaps best positioned to counteract biases and exert influence over perpetrators.[37] Organizations can help members learn about and name microaggressions and how they function by investing in trainings as well as support as people learn effective ways to interrupt and change patterns of behavior. This type of training and support can be particularly helpful for targets of microaggressions by legitimizing their experiences and disrupting any ambiguity around them.[38] These trainings should be ongoing, as research suggests their positive impact can fade over time when not attended to regularly.[39]

How can bystanders and allies best intervene in microaggressions? Sue and colleagues suggest it is important to first disarm the microaggression. Some strategies to do this include expressing disagreement ("I don't find that funny at all, and I don't want to hear jokes like that in the future"), challenging what was said or done ("I wonder if Stephanie would like to finish her thought as she was interrupted?"), or pointing out its harmful impact ("When you constantly and publicly challenge

Franny's decisions, it suggests a lack of respect for her well-earned exper-tise"). Next, they recommend working to educate the perpetrator by engaging them in a conversation about the relationship between their comments and their assumptions or beliefs about particular groups. This could include appealing to their stated values and principles as well as working to promote their empathy toward and understanding of oth-ers.[40] As discussed by Jasmine D. Williams and colleagues, and given the often-fraught nature of discussions regarding race and racism, sexism, and other forms of discrimination, having these types of conversations requires a culture of psychological safety in which people feel safe to take risks and learn.[41]

Finally, it's important for those fighting microaggressions to seek external reinforcement or support, specifically from those with greater authority and power. This also means that those in authority need to send messages that bigoted behavior will not be tolerated and to align orga-nizational policies with this sentiment. Any actions taken in response to microaggressions must be attentive not simply to interpersonal inter-actions but also to systems-oriented change. This might include a deep and thorough investigation of the hiring, evaluation, promotion, and compensation models in the organization and the degree to which they provide equitable access and outcomes across groups.

CHAPTER SIX

What Now?

In this book, we presented a variety of frameworks and phenomena—emotional labor, the double bind, the glass cliff, and gendered and gendered racial microaggressions—to help explain women's experiences as they attempt to access or work as K–12 education leaders. Specifically, we aimed to illuminate how systems of discrimination operate and reinforce stereotypes and biases about women's fit with, and effectiveness in, leadership roles. We were driven to do so as we believe that the only way we can really ensure that women have equitable opportunities and fully express themselves and their values in these roles is by illuminating such systems, structures, and patterns of behavior that tend to repeat themselves in organizations. We cannot counter what we cannot see, and so we must learn to recognize how gender discrimination and gendered racism is operationalized in everyday life and in school systems in particular.

When we fail to see and acknowledge how such discrimination occurs in everything from mentoring to interview questions to evaluations to when meetings occur and where, we also make it less likely that we will revise or, even better, dismantle, these structures in favor of more equitable ones. Instead, because of a lack of understanding or a willful ignorance on the part of those in power, discriminatory systems remain intact and continue to replicate discriminatory access and outcomes while simultaneously placing the blame on women for these results. As we mention in chapter 3, this phenomenon, called second-generation bias, can manifest in narratives that suggest the lack of representation of women and women of color in various education leadership roles is a function of women opting out or not really having the desire to pursue such roles.[1] Such nonsense then gets peddled through a variety of women's empowerment programming and literature pushing women to have more courage or ambition but never actually helping them to connect to one another or learn how to act against such discrimination in a more systematic way. All the women leaders we know have plenty of courage and ambition; what they don't always have is knowledge about how discrimination operates, specific strategies to deploy to challenge it, or networks of allies ready to work alongside them to elevate their leadership in ways they deserve.

We hope this book has helped you build the necessary knowledge and reflective practice so that you can name some of the discriminatory systems present in your life (or in the lives of those you care for or work with), and that it has provided you with new ways to consider moving forward together. We caution that this work will be challenging—new ways of thinking, like any change, can often come with a sense of loss.

Indeed, as we continue talking about these issues in workshops, in classrooms, and with colleagues, women often tell us that while they are glad to have this new knowledge, it also often makes them feel sad and angry. Their sadness comes with the realization that they have less power in determining their access to and success in leadership than they thought. For many, acceptance of discriminatory systems runs in direct conflict with the belief that education leadership is a meritocracy in which those who are the most deserving and skilled are also those who will be the most successful and earn the best opportunities for influence. This is a manipulative lie that keeps us from examining the impact of discrimination and one that we must unravel to build something better.

Once women go through a period of sadness, they often feel angry as they begin to see how prevalent and persistent gender discrimination and gendered racism are in their daily lives. They get angry too as they think about how many times they or their friends received advice or feedback that did more to keep them in conformance with discriminatory systems than to support their leadership potential and power. Such feelings are normal and actually are a positive first step—a frame that in itself challenges gendered norms of behavior. We encourage women and their allies to sit with the anger and allow it to fuel their planning and actions. Time after time, we have seen women's anger change the world; don't try to get rid of it or push it down. Consider instead how to channel it strategically to bring about change for you and others using some of the approaches we have suggested throughout the book. As Soraya Chemaly, author and activist, tells us,

> In the coming years, we will hear, again, that anger is a destructive force, to be controlled. Watch carefully, because not everyone is asked to do this in equal measure. Women, especially, will be told to set our anger aside in favor of a kinder, gentler approach to change. This is a false juxtaposition. Reenvisioned, anger can be the most feminine of virtues: compassionate, fierce, wise, and powerful. The women I admire most—those who have looked to themselves and the limitations and adversities that come with our bodies and the expectations that come with them—have all found ways to transform their anger into meaningful change. In them, anger has moved from debilitation to liberation.[2]

This liberation is also rooted in women's ability to connect with one another and tell the truth about our experiences. Those benefiting most from discriminatory systems do not want women talking to each other and collectively challenging stereotypes and ways of thinking about leadership as primarily a White, male endeavor. In contrast, what might a world look like in which women are constantly uplifting one another and their skills and joining together to advocate and act for all women and their needs? When women connect, share, and plan for collective action, their power is amplified. Beyond some of the ideas that were present at the end of each chapter, what might such actions look like on an everyday basis? How can we act with agency in a system that wishes us not to? How can we create conditions so women of all identities, and everyone else, can do their best work and thrive? These are the key questions we have long asked in all our work and one we hope you will consider.

AGENCY IN DISCRIMINATORY SYSTEMS

It is critical to understand that a push for understanding and analyzing systems in no way denies or lessens the role of women's or others' agency; however, it does reshape it. We define agency as the ability for someone to initiate and act, ideally without fear of retribution or violence. The first step toward agency is knowledge. If one is unaware or willingly blind to discriminatory systems, the only choice is to act in response to the discrimination. An example of this would be a woman who is constantly told that she is too "emotional" or "passionate" and comes to believe that this is indeed the case and that good leaders should be stoic and thus, removes emotion in her voice and presentation to avoid critique. Alternatively, she may push back and get reprimanded, receiving negative reviews for her performance and potentially internalizing them as true. Acknowledgment of such punishment is in contrast to suggesting that the woman lacks confidence or pathologizing her response as "imposter syndrome." However, if she were to recognize that this construction of leadership is gendered (and often racialized), the definition of leadership being promoted becomes the problem rather than the woman herself.

Recognizing that discriminatory systems exist cannot, in and of itself, make them disappear, nor does that recognition insulate traditionally marginalized groups from discrimination. But it does allow those within these systems to support one another to make choices about how they respond to such systems, including the degree to which they will participate in reinforcing particular beliefs or challenge them (or to create networks and behaviors that can collectively dismantle them). Then, when women face retribution for speaking up and out (as they are likely to do), they can collectively recognize the source of the problem and come together for solidarity and support.

In thinking about these choices, we might imagine them ranging from totally refusing to participate in such systems to outwardly taking on many of the valued attributes of leadership defined by the system. Although we take a position that (1) it's not up to us to judge anyone's approach to survival in a hostile environment and (2) we need people fighting inside, outside, and in between, we tend to counsel toward an approach that challenges the system but does so in ways that allows one to persist within it. This sort of tempered radicalism, in which individuals continuously push for change without fanfare or drama, can be a powerful mechanism for change while helping to ensure that women continue to move up the ladder, gaining greater authority and thus ability to change the system as they do.[3] We don't suggest that women ignore cultural codes, but rather that they treat these codes as suspect and make choices about how much they want to play the game while simultaneously recognizing that the game is rigged and trying to change it. And if this doesn't work, sometimes the best and bravest thing to do is leave a toxic environment (and perhaps hire an attorney).

Jennie can serve as an illustration of the type of agency we advocate for. In addition to her teaching and writing, she has the privilege of serving as an expert witness on gender and racial discrimination in the workplace, and in this role, she is sometimes deposed in court. Jennie feels strongly about challenging the sexist belief that to be taken seriously as professionals women need to wear masculine attire or else be deemed "unprofessional." But when she goes to court, she usually wears a dark blazer. She does this not because she actually believes that this outfit makes her a better or more capable witness, but because she understands that those around her might believe this, and she wants to do everything in her power to ensure that her clients' case is taken seriously. She understands the potential for bias and yet has tried to remain authentic to who she is and will fight to make it even better for other women moving forward.

Indeed, in contexts in which Jennie feels that her expertise is more taken as fact, for example, in her courses, lectures, and consulting work, she takes the calculated risk of wearing what she wants, dying her hair any color she feels like, and otherwise presents in ways she chooses—a privilege that she understands to be more available to her due to other features of her identity (e.g., Whiteness, class, sexual orientation), but still an act of defiance that may help others push against the system, too. More important, she knows that in these cases she is every bit the professional she was when she was wearing her blazer in court. She activates her agency by deciding when and how to fight to accomplish her goals. She tries not to internalize how the system defines her. She persists and works every way she can, including by serving as an expert on discrimination, to move the system forward. Sometimes it works really well and sometimes it's all too much, but she keeps at it. We hope you will, too.

Beyond personal choices, agency in discriminatory systems can also look like micromoves that women or others can take not only to signal that they see the behaviors and systems in play but also to bring about change to those systems. An example of a micromove might be building on a woman's comment in a meeting after a male colleague has tried to restate it as his own. It ensures attribution and amplification—correcting a pattern of discriminatory behavior—without directly confronting the male colleague. Known as "upward voicing," this strategy has been examined in a host of situations in which there is a minority perspective that needs to be heard but tends to be missed.[4]

In addition, microlevel coaching before a meeting can be effective in making sure that a person's voice and expertise are taken seriously. Consider mentioning to other colleagues that you look forward to hearing what Monica has to say in the upcoming meeting or appreciating in a follow-up meeting what Monica shared. Those kinds of pre- and post-micromoves can reinforce the expertise of women who may not have felt or actually been heard when they should have been. Coaching on the way to a meeting or afterward can be effective as well in building a psychologically safe work environment. "I am looking forward to hearing your thoughts" as you walk to a meeting or "I really appreciated your points" as you leave a meeting are minicoaching scenarios that can really help people, of any race, status, or gender, feel more psychologically safe.[5] The latter are private moves, but both private and public moves are important and, over time, they may add up to change the culture to one in which everyone's voice is truly valued.

Some of these micromoves may be more difficult given that people are working in hybrid or remote work environments where it is more difficult to read nonverbal cues or to check in with colleagues about their views on the way to and returning from meetings. Coaching is certainly more difficult on video calls. Building in a "green room" or waiting room can be important or setting up a side-chat may be helpful. In some ways, these new online venues may augment the potential for interruptions and coaching in ways that haven't yet been studied.

As one concrete example, Monica was in an online meeting of a selection committee of five senior people in which she was the only woman. She noticed that the list of candidates that had accumulated in the chat included only one woman out of eight names. Monica raised the common goal of coming up with a diverse candidate pool to nods of agreement from the room and then noted, however, the lack of diversity on the list. Having the data right in front of you can make people's assumptions and missteps much more obvious. It may not stop the discriminatory practice immediately, but it does make it easier to interrupt. Similarly, tools such as note-catchers in breakout groups can create transparency in process and thinking. These are new tools that leaders of all kinds can employ to level the playing field and give more people a voice. Although many of us groan about video meetings and prefer meeting together in person, some of these new ways of working might turn out to be opportunities for women and others to capture a bit of airtime when their voices may otherwise have been silenced.

A NOTE ON ALLYSHIP

As we wrote this book, we went back and forth about whether and to what degree it was our responsibility to try to move men to be better allies to female education leaders. On the one hand, it felt important to ensure that men, and particularly White men, felt invited into the conversation. As those currently with the most power in our institutions, school systems included, they also have the greatest leverage in terms of changing discriminatory practices and policies. On the other hand, it strikes us as highly problematic that the responsibility to convince men to be allies rests on those who are the targets of this discrimination, in this case, women and women of color. In the end, we concluded that it is not our responsibility to convince anyone that our humanity and potential is just as valuable as a man's—though sadly it feels that women must make this argument with greater regularity.

Of course, we want men to be allies. However, we believe that *they need to want it* just as much as we do. They then need to begin the often-difficult process of first educating themselves about issues related to gender discrimination and gendered racism and reflect on their power and privilege relative to this knowledge. Reading this book would be a great first step; however, if one is serious about understanding how gender and gendered racism have long operated in our society, there are many more books to read and people steeped in this work to listen to (we've referenced many of these resources). Male allyship would also mean that men would need to take action by actively working every day to unlearn stereotypes and biases as well as to change policies and structures that reinforce them.[6] Finally, it would require that men change their own behavior and act courageously—sometimes in ways that might feel interpersonally risky as they challenge their and male colleagues' privileged position and power.[7] We encourage all men to take such steps and look forward to when they will stand with us in this work as true partners.

While we don't feel beholden to educating men, we do consider it our duty, because of our own positionality as White women, to call on other White women to be better allies to their sisters of color. You cannot call yourself a feminist or advocate for gender equity if you are not simultaneously advocating for racial equity. It's time to own up and get right on this fact. Therefore, White women, like White men, must go through a process of interrogating Whiteness, which "involves critical reflection about Whiteness and privilege as well as the implications of living and working in a race-centered society."[8] This may be a new process for many, as many White people are not put in the position of thinking about themselves as racialized beings, let alone asked to critically reflect on this fact. Again, we recommend Ella Bell Smith and Stella M. Nkomo's book *Our Separate Ways* as a starting point to better understand common blind spots for White women and their ability to serve as true allies to their female colleagues of color or even women more generally.[9]

This shared reflective practice can help facilitate what Tina Opie and Beth Livingston call a shared sisterhood approach. In shared sisterhood, women with varying racial, ethnic, and other identities can come to build coalitions based on trust, empathy, and risk-taking to build bridges and engage in a collective action.[10] This is a path forward that we wholeheartedly endorse and are working to achieve in our work lives. It is work that White women can take up, and they can begin to do this important self-work to make this a true possibility moving forward.

BROADENING AND NARROWING THE LENS

Through the diverse stories of the women featured in this book, we have provided a number of opportunities for readers to see their and perhaps other female leaders' worlds in new ways. However, we acknowledge that our perspective was limited and encourage others to pick up and extend our efforts. For example, we aimed to use an intersectional framework to guide our efforts, but we acknowledge that there are a number of identities that we neither attended to relative to women in education leadership nor discussed in terms of how they relate to power and privilege in our society. For example, although we tried to be inclusive of all women, we focused our attention on those who identified as cisgendered. We did not explicitly speak to the experiences of our trans sisters and the similar and unique types of discrimination they face in the world and as education leaders. All of the women in our cases also identified as heterosexual, again creating a need for further work on how those identifying as LGBTQI+ and as women are treated on the path to and in education leadership positions. We made the decision to focus on what we know best and on areas where research has been situated, and this book is limited to these topics as a result.

The intersection of gender and other identity markers, such as social class and age, also need to be further explored. Older women, for example, face different kinds of discrimination than their younger colleagues and may also hold caregiving responsibilities that look different, but are no less time-consuming or important. There are various forms of dependent care that we did not explore (e.g., siblings, parents, other family members) but that affect large swaths of women and undoubtedly female education leaders. Indeed, these responsibilities may multiply as women, just as they begin to take on formal leadership positions, find themselves taking on care for their aging parents while still also caring for older children. Additionally, we would suggest that despite our focus on K–12 education leadership in the United States, much of our findings are salient for other educational institutions (early childhood and higher education) and potentially other fields. We certainly do not presuppose that systems of discrimination look the same across different cultural contexts, but we do suggest that some of the frameworks may be applicable in giving name to how discrimination is being operationalized (e.g., different forms of microaggressions, stereotyped roles driving decision-making).

We might also suggest that the ideas in this book can be useful even to those who find themselves in contexts in which women, and others from minoritized groups, have more access to leadership. Although numbers do matter when trying to create greater equity and avoiding tokenism, representation itself does not necessarily mean that discrimination has ceased to exist.[11] You can probably imagine, and perhaps have experienced, female-led organizations that uplift traditional masculine stereotyped agentic behaviors. This might include an orientation toward competition over collaboration and top-down decision-making. Alternatively, we might see organizations that embrace stereotyped feminine attributes, avoiding conflict to the point that a toxic culture of nice or of overwork develops and emotional labor is normalized. Put simply, unless your organization has done active work to name and directly confront gender bias and gendered racism, the composition of leadership bodies may have little impact on how such discrimination operates in the space.

On this note, we offer that even if the specifics of your situation and context may not be perfectly aligned with the cases in this book, we believe there is potential to find meaningful ways to apply the learning within it. The theories and phenomena we presented are shown to exist across organizations—it is education that has been slow to apply them in our context. We hope that you will share this book with others and find points of connection and support as we move forward together.

CONCLUDING THOUGHTS

We have called for an end to rhetoric about women needing to "lean in," which can place the blame, so to speak, on the inaction of the targets of discrimination, rather than the systems and structures in which it takes place. Instead, we suggest that, armed with a deeper understanding of how discrimination functions, women can and should stand tall together. Unfortunately, however, women are often either made to sit down or to feel that they should be sitting down. This needs to change. We believe that women deserve much more than a seat at the table or to bend to a discriminatory system; they deserve to stand tall with and among their male peers. To achieve this, we must take a deep look at our values and assumptions about leadership and how it is enacted in school and school systems.

But ultimately, what matters is not what we believe, but what you believe, what you have experienced, and what resonates for you based on your reading of this book. Our aim has been to offer some concepts and frameworks for you to hang your own experiences on, like a sturdy coatrack. If you had a minor or major "a-ha" when reading these cases, that's wonderful. Cases are often sticky and are somewhat projective. But what you hang on that coatrack and the insights you take with you are up to you.

We hope the questions we provided at the end of the cases will deepen your own reflective practice and help you do some thoughtful diagnosis so that you can figure out why you have felt stuck, perhaps, in your career. Or why, perhaps, you have felt stooped over when you know that you should have stood upright. With knowledge and thoughtful diagnosis, you, as leaders in education, can have the power to have agency, along with others, to stand tall and change those systems, structures, and even others' behaviors. But without awareness, even on our own part, behavior is incredibly difficult to change. We hope that this book offers you some valuable knowledge and insights about how to lead change—not just to shift your own personal work environment but to change the work lives of many who will follow you. As you do this good work in sisterhood with others, we are confident you will have even greater power to thrive and to improve the lives of the children and communities you lead.

Notes

FOREWORD

1. Patricia Palmieri and Charol Smith Shakeshaft, "Up the Front Staircase: A Proposal for Women to Achieve Parity with Men in the Field of Educational Administration," *Journal of the NAWDAC* 38, no. 2 (1976): 58–64.
2. Rudine Sims Bishop, "Walk Tall in the World: African American Literature for Today's Children," *Journal of Negro Education* 59, no. 4 (1990): 556–565.

CHAPTER 1

1. National Center for Education Statistics, *Characteristics of Public School Principals: Condition of Education* (Washington, DC: US Department of Education, Institute of Education Sciences, 2022), https://nces.ed.gov/programs/coe/indicator/cls.
2. April Peters, "Elements of Successful Mentoring of a Female School Leader," *Leadership and Policy in Schools* 9, no. 1 (2010): 108–129.
3. Ellen W. Eckman, "Does Gender Make a Difference? Voices of Male and Female High School Principals," *Planning and Changing* 35 (2004): 192–208; Elizabeth H. Gorman, "Gender Stereotypes, Same-Gender Preferences, and Organizational Variation in the Hiring of Women: Evidence from Law Firms," *American Sociological Review* 70, no. 4 (2005): 702–728; Crystal L. Hoyt, and Jeni L. Burnette, "Gender Bias in Leader Evaluations: Merging Implicit Theories and Role Congruity Perspectives," *Personality and Social Psychology Bulletin* 39, no. 10 (2013): 1306–1319.
4. Herminia Ibarra, Robin Ely, and Deborah Kolb, "Women Rising: The Unseen Barriers," *Harvard Business Review* 91, no. 9 (2013): 60–66.

5. Jennie Miles Weiner, Daron Cyr, and Laura J. Burton, "Microaggressions in Administrator Preparation Programs: How Black Female Participants Experienced Discussions of Identity, Discrimination, and Leadership," *Journal of Research on Leadership Education* 16, no. 1 (2021): 3–29.
6. Alice H. Eagly and Steven J. Karau, "Role Congruity Theory of Prejudice Toward Female Leaders," *Psychological Review* 109, no. 3 (2002): 573; Alice H. Eagly and Linda L. Carli, "The Female Leadership Advantage: An Evaluation of the Evidence," *Leadership Quarterly* 14, no. 6 (2003): 807–834; James Sebastian and Jeong-Mi Moon, "Gender Differences in Participatory Leadership: An Examination of Principals' Time Spent Working with Others," *International Journal of Education Policy and Leadership* 12, no. 8 (2017): n8; Jill Sperandio and Alice LaPier, "Confronting Issues of Gender and Ethnicity: Women's Experiences as Aspiring Urban Principals," *Journal of Research on Leadership Education* 4, no. 4 (2009): 67–95.
7. Whitney Sherman Newcomb and Arielle Niemeyer, "African American Women Principals: Heeding the Call to Serve as Conduits for Transforming Urban School Communities," *International Journal of Qualitative Studies in Education* 28, no. 7 (2015): 786–799; Latish Reed and Andrea E. Evans, "'What You See Is [Not Always] What You Get!' Dispelling Race and Gender Leadership Assumptions," *International Journal of Qualitative Studies in Education* 21, no. 5 (2008): 487–499.
8. Patricia Hill Collins, "Intersectionality's Definitional Dilemmas," *Annual Review of Sociology* 41, no. 1 (2015): 2.
9. Kimberle Crenshaw, "Demarginalizing the Intersection of Race and Sex: A Black Feminist Critique of Antidiscrimination Doctrine, Feminist Theory and Antiracist Politics," *University of Chicago Legal Forum* 1989, no. 1 (1989): 140, 139–167.
10. Angela Harris and Zeus Leonardo, "Intersectionality, Race-Gender Subordination, and Education," *Review of Research in Education* 42, no. 1 (2018): 1–27.
11. Ella Bell Smith and Stella M. Nkomo, *Our Separate Ways, With a New Preface and Epilogue: Black and White Women and the Struggle for Professional Identity* (Cambridge, MA: Harvard Business Press, 2021), 139.
12. Samantha E. Erskine and Diana Bilimoria, "White Allyship of Afro-Diasporic Women in the Workplace: A Transformative Strategy for Organizational Change," *Journal of Leadership and Organizational Studies* 26, no. 3 (2019): 319–338.
13. Gloria Steinem at a speech celebrating fifty years of coeducation at Exeter Academy, April 23, 2021.
14. Rudine Sims Bishop, "Windows and Mirrors: Children's Books and Parallel Cultures," in *California State University Reading Conference: 14th Annual Conference Proceedings* (1990), 3–12.
15. Philomena Essed, *Understanding Everyday Racism: An Interdisciplinary Theory*, vol. 2, Sage Series of Race and Ethnic Relations (Thousand Oaks, CA: Sage, 1991).

16. Arlie Russell Hochschild, *The Managed Heart: The Commercialization of Human Feeling* (Berkeley: University of California Press, 1983); Mary Ellen Guy and Meredith A. Newman, "Women's Jobs, Men's Jobs: Sex Segregation and Emotional Labor," *Public Administration Review* 64, no. 3 (2004): 289–298.

17. Emily Kaplan, "Teaching Your Heart Out: Emotional Labor and the Need for Systemic Change," *Edutopia*, July 19, 2019, https://www.edutopia.org/article/teaching-your-heart-out-emotional-labor-and-need-systemic-change.

18. Cassandra M. Guarino and Victor M. H. Borden, "Faculty Service Loads and Gender: Are Women Taking Care of the Academic Family?," *Research in Higher Education* 58, no. 6 (2017): 672–694; Guy and Newman, "Women's Jobs, Men's Jobs."

19. Laurie A. Rudman and Julie E. Phelan, "Backlash Effects for Disconfirming Gender Stereotypes in Organizations," *Research in Organizational Behavior* 28 (2008): 61–79.

20. Eckman, "Does Gender Make a Difference?"

21. Florence L. De Nmark, "Women, Leadership, and Empowerment," *Psychology of Women Quarterly* 17, no. 3 (1993): 343–356; Ava J. Muñoz et al., "A Study of Female Central Office Administrators and Their Aspirations to the Superintendency," *Educational Management Administration and Leadership* 42, no. 5 (2014): 764–784; Jennie Miles Weiner and Laura J. Burton, "The Double Bind for Women: Exploring the Gendered Nature of Turnaround Leadership in a Principal Preparation Program," *Harvard Educational Review* 86, no. 3 (2016): 339–365.

22. Alice H. Eagly and Wendy Wood, "Social Role Theory," in *Handbook of Theories of Social Psychology*, ed. Paul A. M. Van Lange, Arie W. Kruglanski, and E. Tory Higgins (Los Angeles: Sage, 2012), 458–476.

23. Eagly and Wood, "Social Role Theory."

24. Craig Peck, Ulrich C. Reitzug, and Deborah L. West, "Still Waiting for 'Superprincipal': Examining US Policymaker Expectations for School Principals, 2001–2011," *Education Leadership Review* 14, no. 1 (2013): 58–68.

25. Laura J. Burton and Jennie M. Weiner, "'They Were Really Looking for a Male Leader for the Building': Gender, Identity and Leadership Development in a Principal Preparation Program," *Frontiers in Psychology* 7 (2016): 141.

26. Alice H. Eagly and Steven J. Karau, "Role Congruity Theory of Prejudice Toward Female Leaders," *Psychological Review* 109, no. 3 (2002): 573.

27. Susanne Bruckmüller and Nyla R. Branscombe, "The Glass Cliff: When and Why Women Are Selected as Leaders in Crisis Contexts," *British Journal of Social Psychology* 49, no. 3 (2010): 433–451; Michelle K. Ryan and S. Alexander Haslam, "The Glass Cliff: Evidence That Women Are Over-Represented in Precarious Leadership Positions," *British Journal of Management* 16, no. 2 (2005): 81–90.

28. Michelle K. Ryan and S. Alexander Haslam, "The Glass Cliff: Exploring the Dynamics Surrounding the Appointment of Women to Precarious Leadership Positions," *Academy of Management Review* 32, no. 2 (2007): 549–572.

29. Helen Peterson, "An Academic 'Glass Cliff'? Exploring the Increase of Women in Swedish Higher Education Management," *Athens Journal of Education* 1, no. 1 (2014): 33–44.

30. Frank Brown, "African Americans and School Leadership: An Introduction," *Educational Administration Quarterly* 41, no. 4 (2005): 585–590.

31. Peters, "Elements of Successful Mentoring of a Female School Leader."

32. Robert W. Livingston and Ashleigh Shelby Rosette, "Stigmatization, Subordination, or Marginalization? The Complexity of Social Disadvantage across Gender and Race," in *Inclusive Leadership: Transforming Diverse Lives, Workplaces, and Societies*, ed. Bernardo M. Ferdman, Jeanine Prime, and Ronald E. Riggio (New York: Routledge, 2020), 39–59.

33. Kevin Nadal et al., "A Qualitative Approach to Intersectional Microaggressions: Understanding Influences of Race, Ethnicity, Gender, Sexuality, and Religion," *Qualitative Psychology* 2, no. 2 (2015): 147.

34. Melissa Krull and Jerry Robicheau, "Racial Microaggressions and Racial Battle Fatigue: Work-Life Experiences of Black School Principals," *Journal of Education Human Resources* 38, no. 2 (2020): 301–328; Jennie Miles Weiner, Daron Cyr, and Laura J. Burton, "Microaggressions in Administrator Preparation Programs: How Black Female Participants Experienced Discussions of Identity, Discrimination, and Leadership," *Journal of Research on Leadership Education* 16, no. 1 (2021): 3–29.

35. Derald Wing Sue et al., "Racial Microaggressions in Everyday Life: Implications for Clinical Practice," *American Psychologist* 62, no. 4 (2007): 271.

CHAPTER 2

1. Marcia L. Bellas, "Emotional Labor in Academia: The Case of Professors," *Annals of the American Academy of Political and Social Science* 561, no. 1 (1999): 96–110; Nancy Folbre, "Measuring Care: Gender, Empowerment, and the Care Economy," *Journal of Human Development* 7, no. 2 (2006): 183–199; Simone Ispa-Landa and Sara Thomas, "Race, Gender, and Emotion Work Among School Principals," *Gender and Society* 33, no. 3 (2019): 387–409.

2. V. Spike Peterson, "Rethinking Theory: Inequalities, Informalization and Feminist Quandaries," *International Feminist Journal of Politics* 14, no. 1 (2012): 5–35.

3. Paula England, "Emerging Theories of Care Work," *Annual Review of Sociology* 31 (2005): 381–399.

4. "Women in the Labor Force: A Databook," *BLS Reports*, no. 1097 (Washington, DC: US Bureau of Labor Statistics, March 2022), https://www.bls.gov/opub/reports/womens-databook/2021/home.htm#:~:text=In%202020%2C%20the%20share%20of,of%2060.0%20percent%20in%201999.

5. Kim Parker and Wendy Wang, "Modern Parenthood: Roles of Moms and Dads Converge as They Balance Work and Family," *Pew Research Center's Social and Demographic Trends Project* (March 14, 2013), https://www.pewresearch.org/

social-trends/wp-content/uploads/sites/3/2013/03/FINAL_modern_parent-hood_03-2013.pdf.

6. Lucia Ciciolla and Suniya S. Luthar, "Invisible Household Labor and Ramifications for Adjustment: Mothers as Captains of Households," *Sex Roles* 81, no. 7 (2019): 467–486.

7. Arlie Hochschild and Anne Machung, *The Second Shift: Working Families and the Revolution at Home* (New York: Penguin, 2012).

8. Hochschild and Machung, *The Second Shift*, 8.

9. Hochschild and Machung, *The Second Shift*.

10. Mignon Moore, *Invisible Families: Gay Identities, Relationships, and Motherhood Among Black Women* (Berkeley: University of California Press, 2011).

11. Simon Duncan and Rosalind Edwards, *Lone Mothers, Paid Work and Gendered Moral Rationalities* (New York: Springer, 1999).

12. Judith R. Gordon et al., "Balancing Caregiving and Work: Role Conflict and Role Strain Dynamics," *Journal of Family Issues* 33, no. 5 (2012): 662–689, doi:10.1177/0192513x11425322.

13. Jessica A. Peck, "The Disproportionate Impact of COVID-19 on Women Relative to Men: A Conservation of Resources Perspective," *Gender, Work and Organization, Supplement: Feminist Frontiers* 28, no. S2 (2021): 484–497.

14. *2022 State of the Gender Pay Gap Report* (Seattle, WA: Payscale, 2022), https://www.payscale.com/research-and-insights/gender-pay-gap/.

15. Clare Wenham, Julia Smith, and Rosemary Morgan, "COVID-19: The Gendered Impacts of the Outbreak," *Lancet* 395, no. 10227 (2020): 846–848.

16. Lindsay M. Woodbridge, Byeolbee Um, and David K. Duys, "Women's Experiences Navigating Paid Work and Caregiving During the COVID-19 Pandemic," *Career Development Quarterly* 69, no. 4 (2021): 284–298.

17. Margaret MacDonald and Cher Hill, "The Educational Impact of the Covid-19 Rapid Response on Teachers, Students, and Families: Insights from British Columbia, Canada," *Prospects* 51 (2022): 627–641.

18. Michael W. Apple, "Teaching and 'Women's Work': A Comparative Historical and Ideological Analysis," *Teachers College Record* 86, no. 3 (1985): 455–473; Bruce Carrington and Alastair McPhee, "Boys' 'Underachievement' and the Feminization of Teaching," *Journal of Education for Teaching* 34, no. 2 (2008): 109–120; Dana Goldstein, *The Teacher Wars: A History of America's Most Embattled Profession* (New York: Anchor, 2015).

19. Janet Cornelius, "'We Slipped and Learned to Read': Slave Accounts of the Literacy Process, 1830–1865," *Phylon (1960–)* 44, no. 3 (1983): 171–186; Leo Courbot, "Literate Slaves," in *Fred D'Aguiar and Caribbean Literature* (Leiden, The Netherlands: Brill, 2019), 149–206.

20. Terri N. Watson, "Harlem's 'Motherwork' Post-*Brown*: Implications for Urban School Leaders," *Journal of Educational Administration and History* 52, no. 3 (2020): 244–255.

21. Madeleine R. Grumet, *Bitter Milk: Women and Teaching* (Amherst: University of Massachusetts Press, 1988); Myra H. Strober and David Tyack, "Why Do Women Teach and Men Manage? A Report on Research on Schools," *Signs: Journal of Women in Culture and Society* 5, no. 3 (1980): 494–503.

22. Barbara Nelson, "Teachers' Special Knowledge," *Educational Researcher* 21, no. 9 (1992): 32–33; Kathleen Weiler, "Women's History and the History of Women Teachers," *Journal of Education* 171, no. 3 (1989): 9–30.

23. Goldstein, *The Teacher Wars*.

24. Kathy L. Adams and W. Grant Hambright, "Encouraged or Discouraged? Women Teacher Leaders Becoming Principals," *Clearing House: A Journal of Educational Strategies, Issues and Ideas* 77, no. 5 (2004): 209–212.

25. Apple, "Teaching and 'Women's Work.'"

26. Tondra L. Loder and James P. Spillane, "Is a Principal Still a Teacher? US Women Administrators' Accounts of Role Conflict and Role Discontinuity," *School Leadership and Management* 25, no. 3 (2005): 263–279.

27. Susan Auerbach, "Walking the Walk: Portraits in Leadership for Family Engagement in Urban Schools," *School Community Journal* 19, no. 1 (2009): 9–32; Alice H. Eagly, Mona G. Makhijani, and Bruce G. Klonsky, "Gender and the Evaluation of Leaders: A Meta-Analysis," *Psychological Bulletin* 111, no. 1 (1992): 3–22; Angela Urick and Alex J. Bowers, "What Are the Different Types of Principals Across the United States? A Latent Class Analysis of Principal Perception of Leadership," *Educational Administration Quarterly* 50, no. 1 (2014): 96–134.

28. Peter Glick and Susan T. Fiske, "An Ambivalent Alliance: Hostile and Benevolent Sexism as Complementary Justifications for Gender Inequality," *American Psychologist* 56, no. 2 (2001): 109.

29. Joan K. Monin and Margaret S. Clark, "Why Do Men Benefit More from Marriage Than Do Women? Thinking More Broadly About Interpersonal Processes That Occur Within and Outside of Marriage," *Sex Roles* 65, no. 5 (2011): 320–326.

30. Kathy L. Adams and W. Grant Hambright, "Encouraged or Discouraged? Women Teacher Leaders Becoming Principals," *Clearing House: A Journal of Educational Strategies, Issues and Ideas* 77, no. 5 (2004): 209–212; Jennie Miles Weiner and Laura J. Burton, "The Double Bind for Women: Exploring the Gendered Nature of Turnaround Leadership in a Principal Preparation Program," *Harvard Educational Review* 86, no. 3 (2016): 339–365.

31. Mary Ellen Guy and Meredith A. Newman, "Women's Jobs, Men's Jobs: Sex Segregation and Emotional Labor," *Public Administration Review* 64, no. 3 (2004): 289–298.

32. Stephen Fineman, ed., *Emotion in Organizations* (Thousand Oaks, CA: Sage, 2000); Arlie Hochschild, *The Managed Heart: Commercialization of Human Feeling* (Berkeley: University of California Press, 1983).

33. Hochschild, *The Managed Heart*.

34. Diane Zorn and Megan Boler, "Rethinking Emotions and Educational Leadership," *International Journal of Leadership in Education* 10, no. 2 (2007): 137–151.

35. Jacques Charmes, "The Unpaid Care Work and the Labour Market: An Analysis of Time Use Data Based on the Latest World Compilation of Time-Use Surveys" (Geneva, Switzerland: International Labour Office, 2019); Liana C. Sayer, "Gender, Time and Inequality: Trends in Women's and Men's Paid Work, Unpaid Work and Free Time," *Social Forces* 84, no. 1 (2005): 285–303.
36. Lauren P. Bailes and Sarah Guthery, "Held Down and Held Back: Systematically Delayed Principal Promotions by Race and Gender," *AERA Open* 6, no. 2 (2020): https://doi.org/10.1177/2332858420929298; Laura J. Burton and Jennie M. Weiner, "'They Were Really Looking for a Male Leader for the Building': Gender, Identity and Leadership Development in a Principal Preparation Program," *Frontiers in Psychology* 7 (2016): 141; Jafeth E. Sanchez and Bill Thornton, "Gender Issues in K–12 Educational Leadership," *Advancing Women in Leadership Journal* 30 (2010), https://awl-ojs-tamu.tdl.org/awl/article/view/303.
37. Sharon Mavin, Gina Grandy, and Jannine Williams, "Experiences of Women Elite Leaders Doing Gender: Intra-Gender Micro-Violence Between Women," *British Journal of Management* 25, no. 3 (2014): 439–455.
38. Bellas, "Emotional Labor in Academia"; Folbre, "Measuring Care"; Ispa-Landa and Thomas, "Race, Gender, and Emotion Work Among School Principals."
39. Eve Rodsky, *Fair Play: A Game-Changing Solution for When You Have Too Much to Do (and More Life to Live)* (New York: Penguin, 2021).
40. Iris Bohnet, *What Works: Gender Equality by Design* (Cambridge, MA: Harvard University Press, 2016).
41. Bailes and Guthery, "Held Down and Held Back"; Jeannie Myung, Susanna Loeb, and Eileen Horng, "Tapping the Principal Pipeline: Identifying Talent for Future School Leadership in the Absence of Formal Succession Management Programs," *Educational Administration Quarterly* 47, no. 5 (2011): 695–727.
42. Matthew Clifford, "Hiring Quality School Leaders: Challenges and Emerging Practices," *Quality School Leadership Issue Brief* (Naperville, IL: American Institutes for Research, January 2012), https://www.air.org/sites/default/files/downloads/report/Hiring_Quality_School_Leaders_0.pdf.
43. Clifford, "Hiring Quality School Leaders"; Lauren A. Rivera and Jayanti Owens, "Glass Floors and Glass Ceilings: Sex Homophily and Heterophily in Job Interviews," *Social Forces* 99, no. 4 (2021): 1363–1393.
44. Crystal L. Hoyt and Susan E. Murphy, "Managing to Clear the Air: Stereotype Threat, Women, and Leadership," *Leadership Quarterly* 27, no. 3 (2016): 387–399.
45. Bohnet, *What Works.*

CHAPTER 3

1. Jennie M. Weiner and Sarah L. Woulfin, "Controlled Autonomy: Novice Principals' Schema for District Control and School Autonomy," *Journal of Educational Administration* 55, no. 3 (2017): 334–350.

2. Christopher Day and Qing Gu, "Variations in the Conditions for Teachers' Professional Learning and Development: Sustaining Commitment and Effectiveness over a Career," *Oxford Review of Education* 33, no. 4 (2007): 423–443; Linda Evans, "The 'Shape' of Teacher Professionalism in England: Professional Standards, Performance Management, Professional Development and the Changes Proposed in the 2010 White Paper," *British Educational Research Journal* 37, no. 5 (2011): 851–870; Corrie Stone-Johnson and Jennie Weiner, "Theorizing School Leadership as a Profession: A Qualitative Exploration of the Work of School Leaders," *Journal of Educational Administration* 60, no. 4 (2022): 386–402.

3. Lesli A. Maxwell, "The Pandemic May Drive Principals to Quit," *Education Week* (August 21, 2020), https://www.edweek.org/leadership/the-pandemic-may-drive-principals-to-quit/2020/08.

4. Ashley Woo and Elizabeth D. Steiner, *The Well-Being of Secondary School Principals One Year into the COVID-19 Pandemic* (Santa Monica, CA: RAND, 2022), https://www.rand.org/pubs/research_reports/RRA827-6.html.

5. Jennie Miles Weiner and Laura J. Burton, "The Double Bind for Women: Exploring the Gendered Nature of Turnaround Leadership in a Principal Preparation Program," *Harvard Educational Review* 86, no. 3 (2016): 339–365.

6. Tiffany S. Aaron, "Black Women: Perceptions and Enactments of Leadership," *Journal of School Leadership* 30, no. 2 (2020): 146–165.

7. Christine L. Williams, "The Glass Escalator: Hidden Advantages for Men in the 'Female' Professions," *Social Problems* 39, no. 3 (1992): 253–267.

8. Philip Hallinger and Kenneth Leithwood, "Unseen Forces: The Impact of Social Culture on School Leadership," *Peabody Journal of Education* 73, no. 2 (1998): 126–151; Alice H. Eagly, Steven J. Karau, and Blair T. Johnson, "Gender and Leadership Style Among School Principals: A Meta-Analysis," *Educational Administration Quarterly* 28, no. 1 (1992): 76–102.

9. Alice H. Eagly and Steven J. Karau, "Role Congruity Theory of Prejudice Toward Female Leaders," *Psychological Review* 109, no. 3 (2002): 573–598.

10. Ashleigh Shelby Rosette et al., "Race Matters for Women Leaders: Intersectional Effects on Agentic Deficiencies and Penalties," *Leadership Quarterly* 27, no. 3 (2016): 429–445.

11. A. J. Thomas, K. M. Witherspoon, and S. L. Speight, "Gendered Racism, Psychological Distress, and Coping Styles of African American Women," *Cultural Diversity and Ethnic Minority Psychology* 14, no. 4 (2008): 307–314.

12. Robert W. Livingston, Ashleigh Shelby Rosette, and Ella F. Washington, "Can an Agentic Black Woman Get Ahead? The Impact of Race and Interpersonal Dominance on Perceptions of Female Leaders," *Psychological Science* 23, no. 4 (2012): 354–358.

13. J. S. Brooks and G. Jean-Marie, "Black Leadership, White Leadership: Race and Race Relations in an Urban High School," *Journal of Educational Administration*

45, no. 6 (2007): 756–768; Latish Cherie Reed, "The Intersection of Race and Gender in School Leadership for Three Black Female Principals," *International Journal of Qualitative Studies in Education* 25, no. 1 (2012): 39–58.

14. Geert Hofstede, *Culture's Consequences: International Differences in Work-Related Values*, vol. 5 (Beverly Hills, CA: Sage, 1984).

15. Kiyoshi Takahashi, Jun Ishikawa, and Toshihiro Kanai, "Qualitative and Quantitative Studies of Leadership in Multinational Settings: Meta-Analytic and Cross-Cultural Reviews," *Journal of World Business* 47, no. 4 (2012): 530–538.

16. Judy A. Alston, "Tempered Radicals and Servant Leaders: Black Females Persevering in the Superintendency," *Educational Administration Quarterly* 41, no. 4 (2005): 675–688.

17. Craig Peck, Ulrich C. Reitzug, and Deborah L. West, "Still Waiting for 'Super-principal': Examining US Policymaker Expectations for School Principals, 2001–2011," *Education Leadership Review* 14, no. 1 (2013): 58–68.

18. Eagly and Karau, "Role Congruity Theory," 573.

19. Rosette et al., "Race Matters for Women Leaders," 429–445.

20. Wendy Wood and Alice H. Eagly, "Biosocial Construction of Sex Differences and Similarities in Behavior," in *Advances in Experimental Social Psychology*, vol. 46, ed. Mark P. Zanna and James M. Olson (Cambridge, MA: Academic Press, 2012), 55–123.

21. Melissa V. Harris-Perry, *Sister Citizen: Shame, Stereotypes, and Black Women in America* (New Haven, CT: Yale University Press, 2011).

22. Virginia E. Schein et al., "Think Manager—Think Male: A Global Phenomenon?," *Journal of Organizational Behavior* 17, no. 1 (1996): 33–41.

23. Sabine Sczesny, "A Closer Look Beneath the Surface: Various Facets of the Think-Manager–Think-Male Stereotype," *Sex Roles* 49, no. 7 (2003): 353–363.

24. Weiner and Burton, "The Double Bind for Women," 339–365; Laura J. Burton and Jennie M. Weiner, "'They Were Really Looking for a Male Leader for the Building': Gender, Identity and Leadership Development in a Principal Preparation Program," *Frontiers in Psychology* 7 (2016): 141.

25. Jeannie Myung, Susanna Loeb, and Eileen Horng, "Tapping the Principal Pipeline: Identifying Talent for Future School Leadership in the Absence of Formal Succession Management Programs," *Educational Administration Quarterly* 47, no. 5 (2011): 695–727.

26. Eagly and Karau, "Role Congruity Theory," 573.

27. Madeline E. Heilman and Tyler G. Okimoto, "Why Are Women Penalized for Success at Male Tasks? The Implied Communality Deficit," *Journal of Applied Psychology* 92, no. 1 (2007): 81–92; Madeline E. Heilman et al., "Penalties for Success: Reactions to Women Who Succeed at Male Gender-Typed Tasks," *Journal of Applied Psychology* 89, no. 3 (2004): 416–427.

28. Linda L. Carli and Alice H. Eagly, "Gender, Hierarchy, and Leadership: An Introduction," *Journal of Social Issues* 57, no. 4 (2001): 629–636.

29. Laurie A. Rudman and Peter Glick, "Feminized Management and Backlash Toward Agentic Women: The Hidden Costs to Women of a Kinder, Gentler Image of Middle Managers," *Journal of Personality and Social Psychology* 77, no. 5 (1999): 1004–1010.

30. Rudman and Glick, "Feminized Management and Backlash Toward Agentic Women."

31. Herminia Ibarra, Robin Ely, and Deborah Kolb, "Women Rising: The Unseen Barriers," *Harvard Business Review* 91, no. 9 (2013): 60–66.

32. Weiner and Burton, "The Double Bind for Women," 339–365.

33. Eagly and Karau, "Role Congruity Theory," 573.

34. Cassandra M. Guarino and Victor M. H. Borden, "Faculty Service Loads and Gender: Are Women Taking Care of the Academic Family?," *Research in Higher Education* 58, no. 6 (2017): 672–694.

35. Rosette et al., "Race Matters for Women Leaders," 429–445.

36. Sheryl Boris-Schacter and Sondra Langer, *Balanced Leadership: How Effective Principals Manage Their Work* (New York: Teachers College Press, 2006).

37. Sylvia Méndez-Morse, "Chicana Feminism and Education leadership," in *Reconsidering Feminist Research in Education Leadership*, ed. Michelle D. Young and Linda Skrla (Albany: State University of New York Press, 2003), 161–178.

38. Jia "Grace" Liang and April L. Peters-Hawkins, "'I Am More Than What I Look Alike': Asian American Women in Public School Administration," *Educational Administration Quarterly* 53, no. 1 (2017): 46.

39. Jioni A. Lewis et al., "'Ain't I a Woman?' Perceived Gendered Racial Microaggressions Experienced by Black Women," *Counseling Psychologist* 44, no. 5 (2016): 758–780.

40. Ibarra, Ely, and Kolb, "Women Rising," 64.

41. Owen Dyer, "Covid-19: Projections of Mortality in the US Rise as States Open up," *BMJ* 369, m1846 (2020), doi:10.1136/bmj.m1846.

42. Aaron, "Black Women," 146–165.

43. Robin J. Ely, Herminia Ibarra, and Deborah M. Kolb, "Taking Gender into Account: Theory and Design for Women's Leadership Development Programs," *Academy of Management Learning and Education* 10, no. 3 (2011): 474–493.

44. Ibarra, Ely, and Kolb, "Women Rising," 60–66.

45. Ibarra, Ely, and Kolb, "Women Rising," 66.

46. Ibarra, Ely, and Kolb, "Women Rising," 64.

47. Iris Bohnet, *What Works: Gender Equality by Design* (Cambridge, MA: Harvard University Press, 2016), 17.

48. Eagly and Karau, "Role Congruity Theory," 591.

CHAPTER 4

1. Michelle K. Ryan and S. Alexander Haslam, "The Glass Cliff: Evidence That Women Are Over-Represented in Precarious Leadership Positions," *British Journal of Management* 16, no. 2 (2005): 81–90.

2. Susanne Bruckmüller and Nyla R. Branscombe, "The Glass Cliff: When and Why Women Are Selected as Leaders in Crisis Contexts," *British Journal of Social Psychology* 49, no. 3 (2010): 433–451.

3. Michelle K. Ryan and S. Alexander Haslam, "The Glass Cliff: Exploring the Dynamics Surrounding the Appointment of Women to Precarious Leadership Positions," *Academy of Management Review* 32, no. 2 (2007): 549–572; Michelle K. Ryan et al., "Getting on Top of the Glass Cliff: Reviewing a Decade of Evidence, Explanations, and Impact," *Leadership Quarterly* 27, no. 3 (2016): 446–455.

4. Victoria L. Brescoll, Erica Dawson, and Eric Luis Uhlmann, "Hard Won and Easily Lost: The Fragile Status of Leaders in Gender-Stereotype-Incongruent Occupations," *Psychological Science* 21, no. 11 (2010): 1640–1642.

5. Stephen P. Ferris, Murali Jagannathan, and Adam C. Pritchard, "Too Busy to Mind the Business? Monitoring by Directors with Multiple Board Appointments," *Journal of Finance* 58, no. 3 (2003): 1087–1111.

6. Alison Cook and Christy Glass, "Women and Top Leadership Positions: Towards an Institutional Analysis," *Gender, Work and Organization* 21, no. 1 (2014): 91–103.

7. Ryan and Haslam, "The Glass Cliff: Exploring the Dynamics Surrounding the Appointment of Women," 555.

8. Debra L. Nelson and Ronald J. Burke, "Women Executives: Health, Stress, and Success," *Academy of Management Perspectives* 14, no. 2 (2000): 107–121.

9. Ryan and Haslam, "The Glass Cliff: Exploring the Dynamics Surrounding the Appointment of Women," 555.

10. Susanne Bruckmüller et al., "Beyond the Glass Ceiling: The Glass Cliff and Its Lessons for Organizational Policy," *Social Issues and Policy Review* 8, no. 1 (2014): 202–232; Ryan et al., "Getting on Top of the Glass Cliff"; Amy E. Smith, "On the Edge of a Glass Cliff: Women in Leadership in Public Organizations," *Public Administration Quarterly* 39, no. 3 (2015): 484–517.

11. Helen Peterson, "Is Managing Academics 'Women's Work'? Exploring the Glass Cliff in Higher Education Management," *Educational Management Administration and Leadership* 44, no. 1 (2016): 112–127.

12. Corrie Stone-Johnson and Jennie Weiner, "Theorizing School Leadership as a Profession: A Qualitative Exploration of the Work of School Leaders," *Journal of Educational Administration* 60, no. 4 (2022): 386–402.

13. Jennie Miles Weiner, "From New to Nuanced: (Re)Considering Educator Professionalism and Its Impacts," *Journal of Educational Change* 21, no. 3 (2020): 443–454.

14. Smith, "On the Edge of a Glass Cliff."

15. Frank Brown, "African Americans and School Leadership: An Introduction," *Educational Administration Quarterly* 41, no. 4 (2005): 585–590.

16. April Peters, "Elements of Successful Mentoring of a Female School Leader," *Leadership and Policy in Schools* 9, no. 1 (2010): 108–129.

17. Ashleigh Shelby Rosette and Robert W. Livingston, "Failure Is Not an Option for Black Women: Effects of Organizational Performance on Leaders with Single Versus Dual-Subordinate Identities," *Journal of Experimental Social Psychology* 48, no. 5 (2012): 1162–1167.

18. Bruckmüller et al., "Beyond the Glass Ceiling," 202–232.

19. Bruckmüller and Branscombe, "The Glass Cliff," 433–451.

20. Michelle K. Ryan, S. Alexander Haslam, and Tom Postmes, "Reactions to the Glass Cliff: Gender Differences in the Explanations for the Precariousness of Women's Leadership Positions," *Journal of Organizational Change Management* 20, no. 2 (2007): 182–197.

21. Ellen W. Eckman, "Does Gender Make a Difference? Voices of Male and Female High School Principals," *Planning and Changing* 35 (2004): 192–208; Jennie Miles Weiner and Laura J. Burton, "The Double Bind for Women: Exploring the Gendered Nature of Turnaround Leadership in a Principal Preparation Program," *Harvard Educational Review* 86, no. 3 (2016): 339–365.

22. Michelle K. Ryan et al., "Opting Out or Pushed Off the Edge? The Glass Cliff and the Precariousness of Women's Leadership Positions," *Social and Personality Psychology Compass* 1, no. 1 (2007): 266–279; Ryan, Haslam, and Postmes, "Reactions to the Glass Cliff," 182–197.

23. Bruckmüller et al., "Beyond the Glass Ceiling," 202–232.

24. Peterson, "Is Managing Academics 'Women's Work'?"

25. Michelle K. Ryan et al., "Getting on Top of the Glass Cliff: Reviewing a Decade of Evidence, Explanations, and Impact," *Leadership Quarterly* 27, no. 3 (2016): 451.

26. Linda L. Carli and Alice H. Eagly, "Gender, Hierarchy, and Leadership: An Introduction," *Journal of Social Issues* 57, no. 4 (2001): 629–636.

27. Michelle K. Ryan et al., "Think Crisis–Think Female: The Glass Cliff and Contextual Variation in the Think Manager–Think Male Stereotype," *Journal of Applied Psychology* 96, no. 3 (2011): 470–484.

28. Bruckmüller et al., "Beyond the Glass Ceiling," 202–232.

29. This uplift of female leaders was featured prominently during the peak of the COVID-19 crisis in the media. While we are perfectly comfortable with celebrating the accomplishments and hard work of women like Angela Merkel, Jacinda Arden, and so many others, we argue that the framing of these stories—that being a woman itself is the reason for their success—serves to reinforce stereotypes and limits the band of permissible behavior female leaders can use. The portrayal is also somewhat disingenuous in that there were plenty of female leaders (many in the United States) who did little to thoughtfully protect their citizens from the pandemic (we leave it up to you to decide who they might be).

30. Bruckmüller et al., "Beyond the Glass Ceiling," 202–232.

31. Ryan et al., "Getting on Top of the Glass Cliff," 446–455.

32. Gloria Ladson-Billings, "From the Achievement Gap to the Education Debt: Understanding Achievement in US Schools," *Educational Researcher* 35, no. 7 (2006): 3–12.

33. Latish Cherie Reed, "The Intersection of Race and Gender in School Leadership for Three Black Female Principals," *International Journal of Qualitative Studies in Education* 25, no. 1 (2012): 39–58; Jennie Weiner, Daron Cyr, and Laura J. Burton, "A Study of Black Female Principals Leading Through Twin Pandemics," *Journal of Education Human Resources* 40, no. 3 (2022): 335–359.

34. Peters, "Elements of Successful Mentoring"; Jennie Miles Weiner and Laura J. Burton, "The Double Bind for Women: Exploring the Gendered Nature of Turnaround Leadership in a Principal Preparation Program," *Harvard Educational Review* 86, no. 3 (2016): 339–365.

35. Ryan et al., "Getting on Top of the Glass Cliff."

36. Ryan et al., "Getting on Top of the Glass Cliff."

37. Ryan and Haslam, "The Glass Cliff: Exploring the Dynamics Surrounding the Appointment of Women."

CHAPTER 5

1. Kevin L. Nadal et al., "A Qualitative Approach to Intersectional Microaggressions: Understanding Influences of Race, Ethnicity, Gender, Sexuality, and Religion," *Qualitative Psychology* 2, no. 2 (2015): 147.

2. Michelle C. Haynes-Baratz et al., "Challenging Gendered Microaggressions in the Academy: A Social–Ecological Analysis of Bystander Action Among Faculty," *Journal of Diversity in Higher Education* 15, no. 4 (2022): 521–535; Mary P. Rowe, "Barriers to Equality: The Power of Subtle Discrimination to Maintain Unequal Opportunity," *Employee Responsibilities and Rights Journal* 3, no. 2 (1990): 153–163.

3. Keeley Hynes et al., "Post or Protest? Factors Influencing White Women's Engagement in Activism," *Journal of Human Behavior in the Social Environment* (2022): 1–13; Jioni A. Lewis et al., "Coping with Gendered Racial Microaggressions Among Black Women College Students," *Journal of African American Studies* 17, no. 1 (2013): 51–73; Jioni A. Lewis et al., "'Ain't I a Woman?' Perceived Gendered Racial Microaggressions Experienced by Black Women," *Counseling Psychologist* 44, no. 5 (2016): 758–780; Kevin L. Nadal et al., "Sexual Orientation Microaggressions: 'Death by a Thousand Cuts' for Lesbian, Gay, and Bisexual Youth," *Journal of LGBT Youth* 8, no. 3 (2011): 234–259; Chester Pierce, "Offensive Mechanisms," in *The Black Seventies*, ed. Floyd Barbour (Boston: Sargent, 1970), 265–282; Derald Wing Sue et al., "Racial Microaggressions in Everyday Life: Implications for Clinical Practice," *American Psychologist* 62, no. 4 (2007): 271–286.

4. Laura J. Burton, Daron Cyr, and Jennie Miles Weiner, "'Unbroken, but Bent': Gendered Racism in School Leadership," *Frontiers in Education* 5 (2020): 52.

5. Peggy C. Davis, "Law as Microaggression," *Yale Law Journal* 98, no. 8 (1989): 1559–1577; Chester M. Pierce, ed., *Television and Education* (Beverly Hills, CA: Sage, 1978).

6. In our discussions with education leaders across gender identities, we find that it is mostly women, from their twenties to late forties, who receive comments regarding their relative youthfulness. We see such comments as more of a general expression of surprise that they, a woman below retirement age, have truly earned and can fulfill such a position. Richard Delgado and Jean Stefancic, "An Introduction to Critical Race Theory," in *Critical Race Theory: The Cutting Edge*, ed. Richard Delgado and Jean Stefancic (Philadelphia, PA: Temple University, 2001), 1–167; Sue et al., "Racial Microaggressions in Everyday Life."

7. Janice McCabe, "Racial and Gender Microaggressions on a Predominantly-White Campus: Experiences of Black, Latina/o and White Undergraduates," *Race, Gender and Class* 16, no. 1/2 (2009): 133–151.

8. Lewis et al., "'Ain't I a Woman?'"; Kevin L. Nadal, Avy Skolnik, and Yinglee Wong, "Interpersonal and Systemic Microaggressions Toward Transgender People: Implications for Counseling," *Journal of LGBT Issues in Counseling* 6, no. 1 (2012): 55–82; Kevin L. Nadal, *That's So Gay! Microaggressions and the Lesbian, Gay, Bisexual, and Transgender Community* (Washington, DC: American Psychological Association, 2013); Kevin L. Nadal et al., "Racial Microaggressions and Asian Americans: An Exploratory Study on Within-Group Differences and Mental Health," *Asian American Journal of Psychology* 6, no. 2 (2015): 136–144; Marlene G. Williams and Jioni A. Lewis, "Gendered Racial Microaggressions and Depressive Symptoms Among Black Women: A Moderated Mediation Model," *Psychology of Women Quarterly* 43, no. 3 (2019): 368–380.

9. We focus on these groups neither to suggest that they are monolithic nor that other intersecting identities are of less interest or import. Rather we do so because they are currently those for which we could find robust research with regards to their experiences with microaggressions.

10. Sue et al., "Racial Microaggressions in Everyday Life"; Rachel Endo, "How Asian American Female Teachers Experience Racial Microaggressions from Pre-Service Preparation to Their Professional Careers," *Urban Review* 47, no. 4 (2015): 601–625; Malik S. Henfield, "Black Male Adolescents Navigating Microaggressions in a Traditionally White Middle School: A Qualitative Study," *Journal of Multicultural Counseling and Development* 39, no. 3 (2011): 141–155.

11. Nadal et al., "Sexual Orientation Microaggressions," 234.

12. Jioni A. Lewis and Helen A. Neville, "Construction and Initial Validation of the Gendered Racial Microaggressions Scale for Black Women," *Journal of Counseling Psychology* 62, no. 2 (2015): 289–302; Rachel Elizabeth Gartner, *From Gender Microaggressions to Sexual Assault: Measure Development and Preliminary Trends Among Undergraduate Women* (PhD diss., University of California,

Berkeley, 2019); Anahvia Taiyib Moody and Jioni A. Lewis, "Gendered Racial Microaggressions and Traumatic Stress Symptoms Among Black Women," *Psychology of Women Quarterly* 43, no. 2 (2019): 201–214; Kevin L. Nadal et al., "Gender Microaggressions: Perceptions, Processes, and Coping Mechanisms of Women," *Psychology for Business Success* 1 (2013): 193–220; Williams and Lewis, "Gendered Racial Microaggressions and Depressive Symptoms Among Black Women"; LaTrice N. Wright and Jioni A. Lewis, "Is Physical Activity a Buffer? Gendered Racial Microaggressions and Anxiety Among African American Women," *Journal of Black Psychology* 46, no. 2–3 (2020): 122–143.

13. Tessa E. Basford, Lynn R. Offermann, and Tara S. Behrend, "Do You See What I See? Perceptions of Gender Microaggressions in the Workplace," *Psychology of Women Quarterly* 38, no. 3 (2014): 340–349; Burton, Cyr, and Weiner, "'Unbroken, but Bent.'"

14. Basford, Offermann, and Behrend, "Do You See What I See?," 341; Lindsay Pérez Huber and Daniel G. Solorzano, "Racial Microaggressions as a Tool for Critical Race Research," *Race Ethnicity and Education* 18, no. 3 (2015): 297–320; Valerie Purdie-Vaughns and Richard P. Eibach, "Intersectional Invisibility: The Distinctive Advantages and Disadvantages of Multiple Subordinate-Group Identities," *Sex Roles* 59, no. 5 (2008): 377–391; Sue et al., "Racial Microaggressions in Everyday Life."

15. Christina M. Capodilupo et al., "The Manifestation of Gender Microaggressions," in *Microaggressions and Marginality: Manifestation, Dynamics, and Impact*, ed. D. W. Sue (New York: Wiley, 2010), 193–216.

16. Jason A. Grissom et al., "Unequal Pay for Equal Work? Unpacking the Gender Gap in Principal Compensation," *Economics of Education Review* 82 (2021): 102–114.

17. Veronica E. Johnson et al., "'It's Not in Your Head': Gaslighting,'Splaining, Victim Blaming, and Other Harmful Reactions to Microaggressions," *Perspectives on Psychological Science* 16, no. 5 (2021): 1024–1036.

18. Meera E. Deo, "The Ugly Truth about Legal Academia," *Brooklyn Law Review* 80, no. 3 (2014): 943–1014.

19. Karen B. Schmaling, "Gender Microaggressions in Higher Education: Proposed Taxonomy and Change Through Cognitive-Behavioral Strategies," *Forum on Public Policy Online* 3, no. 3 (2007).

20. Anita Jones Thomas, Karen M. Witherspoon, and Suzette L. Speight, "Gendered Racism, Psychological Distress, and Coping Styles of African American Women," *Cultural Diversity and Ethnic Minority Psychology* 14, no. 4 (2008): 307–314; Leah R. Warner, "A Best Practices Guide to Intersectional Approaches in Psychological Research," *Sex Roles* 59, no. 5 (2008): 454–463; Gordon B. Willis, *Analysis of the Cognitive Interview in Questionnaire Design* (Oxford: Oxford University Press, 2015).

21. Lewis and Neville, "Construction and Initial Validation of the Gendered Racial Microaggressions Scale for Black Women," 289.
22. Alexcia M. Kilgore, Rachel Kraus, and Linh Nguyen Littleford, "'But I'm Not Allowed to Be Mad': How Black Women Cope with Gendered Racial Microaggressions Through Writing," *Translational Issues in Psychological Science* 6, no. 4 (2020): 372–382.
23. Cecile A. Gadson and Jioni A. Lewis, "Devalued, Overdisciplined, and Stereotyped: An Exploration of Gendered Racial Microaggressions Among Black Adolescent Girls," *Journal of Counseling Psychology* 69, no. 1 (2022): 14–26; Lewis et al., "'Ain't I a Woman?'"
24. Tiffany S. Aaron, "Black Women: Perceptions and Enactments of Leadership," *Journal of School Leadership* 30, no. 2 (2020): 146–165; April L. Peters, "Leading Through the Challenge of Change: African-American Women Principals on Small School Reform," *International Journal of Qualitative Studies in Education* 25, no. 1 (2012): 23–38; Latish Cherie Reed, "The Intersection of Race and Gender in School Leadership for Three Black Female Principals," *International Journal of Qualitative Studies in Education* 25, no. 1 (2012): 39–58.
25. Jennie Miles Weiner, Daron Cyr, and Laura J. Burton, "Microaggressions in Administrator Preparation Programs: How Black Female Participants Experienced Discussions of Identity, Discrimination, and Leadership," *Journal of Research on Leadership Education* 16, no. 1 (2021): 3–29.
26. Brian TaeHyuk Keum et al., "Gendered Racial Microaggressions Scale for Asian American Women: Development and Initial Validation," *Journal of Counseling Psychology* 65, no. 5 (2018): 571–585.
27. Christopher T. H. Liang, Lisa C. Li, and Bryan S. K. Kim, "The Asian American Racism-Related Stress Inventory: Development, Factor Analysis, Reliability, and Validity," *Journal of Counseling Psychology* 51, no. 1 (2004): 103–114.
28. Sue et al., "Racial Microaggressions in Everyday Life."
29. Lindsay Pérez Huber, "Discourses of Racist Nativism in California Public Education: English Dominance as Racist Nativist Microaggressions," *Educational Studies* 47, no. 4 (2011): 379–401.
30. Tara Yosso et al., "Critical Race Theory, Racial Microaggressions, and Campus Racial Climate for Latina/o Undergraduates," *Harvard Educational Review* 79, no. 4 (2009): 659–691.
31. Kevin L. Nadal et al., "Microaggressions and Latina/o Americans: An Analysis of Nativity, Gender, and Ethnicity," *Journal of Latina/o Psychology* 2, no. 2 (2014): 67–78; Deborah S. Peterson and Victor Vergara, "Thriving in School Leadership: Latina/o Leaders Speak Out," *National Forum of Educational Administration and Supervision Journal* 34, no. 4 (2016): 2–15; David P. Rivera, Erin E. Forquer, and Rebecca Rangel, "Microaggressions and the Life Experience of Latina/o

Americans," in *Microaggressions and Marginality: Manifestation, Dynamics, and Impact*, ed. D. W. Sue (New York: Wiley, 2010), 59–83.

32. Sue et al., "Racial Microaggressions in Everyday Life."

33. Kevin L. Nadal et al., "Gender Microaggressions: Perceptions, Processes, and Coping Mechanisms of Women," in *Psychology for Business Success*, ed. M. A. Paludi (Santa Barbara, CA: Praeger, 2013), 1:193–220.

34. Cheryl R. Kaiser and Carol T. Miller, "Stop Complaining! The Social Costs of Making Attributions to Discrimination," *Personality and Social Psychology Bulletin* 27, no. 2 (2001): 254–263; Cheryl R. Kaiser and Carol T. Miller, "Derogating the Victim: The Interpersonal Consequences of Blaming Events on Discrimination," *Group Processes and Intergroup Relations* 6, no. 3 (2003): 227–237.

35. Derald Wing Sue et al., "Racial Microaggressions Against Black Americans: Implications for Counseling," *Journal of Counseling and Development* 86, no. 3 (2008): 330–338.

36. Derald Wing Sue et al., "Disarming Racial Microaggressions: Microintervention Strategies for Targets, White Allies, and Bystanders," *American Psychologist* 74, no. 1 (2019): 128–142.

37. Meg A. Bond and Michelle C. Haynes-Baratz, "Mobilizing Bystanders to Address Microaggressions in the Workplace: The Case for a Systems-Change Approach to Getting a (Collective) GRIP," *American Journal of Community Psychology* 69, no. 1–2 (2022): 221–238.

38. Sue et al., "Disarming Racial Microaggressions."

39. Haynes-Baratz et al., "Challenging Gendered Microaggressions in the Academy."

40. Sue et al., "Disarming Racial Microaggressions."

41. Jasmine D. Williams, Ashley N. Woodson, and Tanner LeBaron Wallace, "'Can We Say the N-Word?' Exploring Psychological Safety During Race Talk," *Research in Human Development* 13, no.1 (2016): 15–31.

CHAPTER 6

1. Herminia Ibarra, Robin Ely, and Deborah Kolb, "Women Rising: The Unseen Barriers," *Harvard Business Review* 91, no. 9 (2013): 60–66.

2. Soraya Chemaly, *Rage Becomes Her* (New York: Simon and Schuster, 2018), 269.

3. Debra E. Meyerson, "Radical Change, the Quiet Way," *Harvard Business Review* (October 2001), https://hbr.org/2001/10/radical-change-the-quiet-way.

4. Patricia Satterstrom, Michaela Kerrissey, and Julia DiBenigno, "The Voice Cultivation Process: How Team Members Can Help Upward Voice Live on to Implementation," *Administrative Science Quarterly* 66, no. 2 (2021): 380–425.

5. Amy C. Edmondson and Zhike Lei, "Psychological Safety: The History, Renaissance, and Future of an Interpersonal Construct," *Annual Review of Organizational Psychology and Organizational Behavior* 1, no. 1 (2014): 23–43.

6. Juliana Carlson et al., "What's in a Name? A Synthesis of 'Allyship' Elements from Academic and Activist Literature," *Journal of Family Violence* 35, no. 8 (2020): 889–898.

7. Elad N. Sherf, Subrahmaniam Tangirala, and Katy Connealy Weber, "It Is Not My Place! Psychological Standing and Men's Voice and Participation in Gender-Parity Initiatives," *Organization Science* 28, no. 2 (2017): 193–210.

8. Diane Grimes, "Putting Our Own House in Order: Whiteness, Change and Organization Studies," *Journal of Organizational Change Management* 14, no. 2 (2001): 134.

9. Ella Bell Smith and Stella M. Nkomo, *Our Separate Ways, With a New Preface and Epilogue: Black and White Women and the Struggle for Professional Identity* (Cambridge, MA: Harvard Business Press, 2021).

10. Tina Opie and Beth Livingston, "Shared Sisterhood™: Harnessing Collective Power to Generate More Inclusive and Equitable Organizations," *Organizational Dynamics* 51, no. 1 (2022): 1–9.

11. Rosabeth Moss Kanter, *Men and Women of the Corporation: New Edition* (New York: Basic Books, 1993).

Acknowledgments

JENNIE WEINER

I would like to thank all of the women K–12 education leaders who have honored us by sharing with us their triumphs, challenges, and everything in between. Your stories matter and we are privileged to learn from them and allow others to as well. On this note, I want to give special recognition to the women of the Connecticut Association of Public School Superintendents (CAPSS) Women's Group, who invited me and my colleague Dr. Laura Burton, another person I owe a huge debt, into their space. The conversations we have engaged in, and the relationships I have built, were key in the development of this book and the insights throughout.

So, too, am I grateful for all of my students at the University of Connecticut, many of whom have worked with me over the years as thought partners and collaborators on this work. A special thank you to Dr. Daron Cyr and Taylor Strickland as well as to Drs. Kimberly Culkin, Shannon Holder, and Alexandra Lamb. I am better for knowing you.

I also have deep affection and appreciation for the students at the Harvard Graduate School of Education who served as the test group for the ideas in this book. They shared themselves and their stories with me—many of which inspired the cases throughout. I want to provide a special thank you to Erica Lim, Kirstin Northenscold, Kari Schuler, Alexis Simpson, and Elena Speridakos for the inspiration they provided for this book and their willingness to engage deeply in our collective learning and growth. You are amazing leaders and women! Thank you for your courage and engagement!

I am blessed to have a number of fierce, brilliant, and supportive mentors and collaborators who have pushed my thinking, given me an ear, and lifted me up when I needed it most. Thank you to Drs. Bianca Montrosse-Moorhead, Sarah Odell, Kerry Robinson, Charol Shakeshaft, Corrie Stone-Johnson, and Suzanne Wilson, for being so wonderful to me and, of course, to Monica Higgins, my coauthor, mentor, friend, and north star.

This book is dedicated to my wonderful friends, powerful women all: Caroline Adler, Sarah Anderson, Andrea Castaneda, Sherry Deckman, Christina Dobbs, Jennifer Dorsey, Chantal Francois, Lisa Goldschmidt, Eliza Johnston, Julianna Kershen, Danielle Rehfeld, Marina Reti, and Elizabeth Shelburne. Keep doing what you're doing—it's working!

Finally, I have the most supportive family. Mom, thank you for being a champion for women, their rights and dreams; you have taught us well. I love you too, Dad, and all you did to raise strong daughters, including my incredible sister Maureen. Michele, thank you for the phone calls and encouragement. Finally, I want to thank Jeremiah, who makes everything possible and more fun and to Manny and Rufus—you are my everything.

MONICA C. HIGGINS

With dedication comes, most of all, gratitude. "What am I most grateful for right now?" It's a question I often ask others. For me, the answer is simple: I am grateful to work with my coauthor and friend, Jennie Weiner, on this book. Although she has been inspired by many and, indeed, so many of her colleagues and our students helped us build the repertoire of cases that have served as the foundation for this book, make no mistake about it: this book would never have happened without her brilliance, perseverance, and determination. Thank you, Jennie, for giving me the opportunity to join you in this writing journey.

I also thank some of my own role models and mentors, including Kathy Kram, who wrote with me and taught me what true mentoring looks like; Rosabeth Moss Kanter, whose work on women in leadership inspired my quest to earn a doctorate in organizational behavior; and Kathy McCartney, whose chair I proudly hold and who was an early sponsor of the *Women in Leadership* program at the Harvard Graduate School of Education, in which Jennie and I both taught and that ignited our desire to write. I am also grateful for my circle of brilliant women friends: Tiziana Casciaro, Becky Coverdale, Amy Edmondson, Laurie Fuller, Jody Hoffer-Gittell, Pamela Kislak, Beth Maloney, Sue Schimmel, and Leslie Tsui. You inspire me.

I also thank and dedicate this book to my mother, Priscilla Claman, who was writing about these issues and counseling women on their careers before I even had a career of my own, and who has always been a thought partner as well as a role model for me in my life. To my father, Vic Claman, who just recently passed, I will always remember how you taught me to love and serve others and to appreciate the beauty in life. To my husband, Michael, thank you for understanding the importance of not just supporting but advocating for women in leadership—for me, for others, and especially for our three strong daughters. To Sarah, Becky, and Mika: I hope that as you explore some of the ideas in this book, you recognize that there is struggle, yes, but there is also so much that we can do together to become a more leader-full society. You are, already, a part of that movement of women who speak up, stand tall, and lift up one another. Thank you for all your support and love.

About the Authors

DR. JENNIE WEINER is an associate professor of educational leadership at the University of Connecticut and was a guest associate professor at the Harvard Graduate School of Education where she taught the course *Women in Educational Leadership* in fall 2020. She is affiliated with UConn's Center for Education Policy Analysis, Research and Evaluation and previously served as the codirector of the school's EdD program. Her scholarship focuses on issues of educational leadership and organizational change, including the impact of gender and racial discrimination in educational leadership. She has presented at national and international conferences, with her work appearing in more than forty peer-reviewed journal articles. She has recently appeared as an expert on issues of women, leadership, and care work for a variety of events and on media outlets, such as *Good Morning America* and *NPR*, as well as on a variety of podcasts. She also facilitates a number of women-focused educational leadership groups (e.g., the Connecticut Female Superintendents Group). In 2017, Dr. Weiner was awarded an Emerging Scholar Award from the American Education Research Association's (AERA) Educational Change (SIG), for which she is chair. She holds an EdD and MEd from the Harvard Graduate School of Education and currently lives with her husband Jeremiah, their twin boys Rufus and Manny, and their dog Junior.

DR. MONICA C. HIGGINS is the Kathleen McCartney Professor of Education Leadership at the Harvard Graduate School of Education (HGSE), where her research and teaching focus on leadership and organizational change. She is also a faculty affiliate at Harvard Kennedy School with the Center for Public Leadership and the Bloomberg Center for Cities and teaches across many of the Harvard Schools in executive programs including *Women in Leadership*. Her recent education research explores the role of psychological safety as reported by teachers in urban public schools and its impact on student learning. Dr. Higgins also conducts research that advances social entrepreneurship in education by leading a Harvard initiative called *Scaling for Impact*, which focuses on helping entrepreneurial leaders scale their work for even greater impact. She co-hosts a podcast called A608 After Hours, that calls in diverse perspectives from the field of education to discuss topics in entrepreneurial leadership. Before joining HGSE in 2006, she spent eleven years on the faculty at Harvard Business School (HBS) where she conducted research on the careers of entrepreneurial leaders, culminating in articles along with a book entitled *Career Imprints: Creating Leaders Across an Industry*. Dr. Higgins also has a twenty-five-year longitudinal multimedia study underway examining the leadership development and career experiences of a group of MBA students from the HBS class of 1996 that has led to business school cases, academic articles, and plans for a documentary. From 2009 to 2016, Dr. Higgins served as an appointee to former Secretary of Education, Arne Duncan, under President Obama. A native New Englander, she enjoys the outdoors in all kinds of weather, running and biking, and spending time with her husband, Michael, her three daughters, Sarah, Becky, and Mika, and their dog, Leo.

Index

Ibarra, Herminia, 2, 49, 66–67
identity
    as Asian American women, 116
    gender, 45
    glass cliff and, 92–93
    intersectionality and, 138
    of leadership, 92
    of LGBTQI+, 138
    of microaggression bystanders, 127
    sexual, 16
    of Weiner, 134
    of women, 3–4, 68
    of women leaders, 2
imposter syndrome, 132
Indigenous children, 17
individualistic culture, 45
in-group favoritism, glass cliff and, 75
institutional bias, prescriptive how-to's
    for, 6
institutional racism
    environmental microaggressions
        and, 124
    against people of color, 93
intersectionality
    feminism and, 4
    gendered microaggressions and, 9
    identity and, 138
    marginalization and, 4
    role congruity theory and, 48–49
interviews, for hiring, 39
in vitro fertilization (IVF), 32

job descriptions, 39
Johnson, Roberta, 77, 87–91,
    93, 94
Jones, Keisha, 76, 77–83, 93
Jordan, Danielle
    role congruity theory and, 49–50,
        55–60
    supervisors of, 68–70

Kim, Josephine (Jo), 20, 27–31, 38
Kolb, Deborah, 2, 49, 66–67
Kwan, Kelly, 106, 113–117
    environmental microaggressions
        against, 124
    microinsults against, 125
    microinvalidations against, 126

Ladson-Billings, Gloria, 93
Latinx. See Hispanic
leadership. See also men leaders;
        women leaders
    identity of, 92
    masculinity and, 46–47
    of men, 43, 131
    servant, 45
    as social construct, 44–45
    stereotypes of, 43, 131–132
    by Whites, 43, 131
Lewis, Jioni A., 104
LGBTQI+
    gendered microaggressions against, 9
    identity of, 138
    microaggressions against, 101
life balance, 15
London Stock Exchange, women
        leaders on, 72–73
lone hero, 7

maleness
    intersectionality and, 4
    in social role theory, 7
marginalization
    gendered microaggressions
        and, 102
    gendered racial microaggressions
        and, 104
    intersectionality and, 4
    microaggressions and, 101